937 wk

Dominic Jan

D1628513

ROMANS AND CHRISTIANS

Dominic Janes

ROMANS AND CHRISTIANS

TEMPUS

First published 2002

PUBLISHED IN THE UNITED KINGDOM BY:

Tempus Publishing Ltd
The Mill, Brimscombe Port
Stroud, Gloucestershire GL5 2QG
www.tempus-publishing.com

PUBLISHED IN THE UNITED STATES OF AMERICA BY:

Tempus Publishing Inc.
2 Cumberland Street
Charleston, SC 29401
1-888-313-2665
www.tempuspublishing.com

British Library Cataloguing in Publication Data.
A catalogue record for this book is available from the British Library.

ISBN 0 7524 1954 4

Typesetting and origination by Tempus Publishing.
PRINTED AND BOUND IN GREAT BRITAIN

Contents

Constantine by Charles Miltenberger, copyright 1990

Preface

I would like to thank Pembroke College in Cambridge, King's College London and the Foundation for International Education which, successively, employed me during the period of gestation of this book. The cost of the illustrations was partly borne by a grant from the Isobel Thornley Bequest Fund of London University. I must thank Duncan Horne for his proof-reading skills. I would also like to thank the artist Charles Miltenberger who provided the frontispiece for this volume. You may see more of his work at www.cmfineart.com. In relation to this image he comments:

> I believe that the process of communicating visually through the medium of oil painting allows a unique opportunity for artist and viewer to meet. As I paint, I never simply copy a scene. My subjects become transcended, acquiring attributes they may not have in real life. If there were nothing more than clever manipulations of paint, I might as well be putting paint on walls instead of on canvas. Imagination is integral to this process. The acts of creating and viewing art are very personal journeys. For me, the image of Constantine and the students is symbolic of the fact that there is as much uniting us over the centuries as dividing us. I hope that viewers will bring their own memories and perceptions to their under-standing of the image.

I strongly believe in examining the past as an exercise in imagination and self-reflection. This book is intended to stimulate that form of engagement. It is not, however, provided with the full apparatus of references which is frequently the weighty accompaniment of academic research. But I shall be delighted to discuss references with readers if they write to me via Tempus Publishing.

Dominic Janes
London 2002

List of illustrations

Unless otherwise indicated, illustrations are from the photographic archive, and by permission, of the German Archaeological Institute in Rome

1 Just another crucifixion

At any single moment there are many hundreds of people being born, procreating and dying. The exact moment of Jesus' death was not so remarkable for the man who had ordered his execution, the Roman governor of Judaea. Pontius Pilate, just like every other Roman dignitary, was perfectly used to sentencing people to death in ways that might now seem bizarre and horrific. His job was to keep public order and the sentence of crucifixion was a standard way of removing troublemakers. Pilate was an equestrian (Roman noble second-class, rich, but not quite a senator) whose later fame is the direct result of his death sentence on Jesus Christ. Otherwise, he was probably an average member of his class and age. I say probably because, as with many important people in the ancient world, we only know him through the reports of others, and not through his own testimony.

Moreover, because we can juxtapose pagan, Jewish and Christian accounts, we find our sources describing three different men. The pagan Pilate was a careerist whose rise and fall mirrored that of his patron Sejanus at the court of the emperor Tiberius. He was ordered back to Rome in 36 for trial on charges of oppression after ordering an attack on a group of Samaritans on Mount Gerizim. But such trials were usually the result of faction fighting in Rome in which otherwise obscure provincial matters could be used as an excuse for personal attacks. The Jewish Pilate appears in the writings of Josephus. He was a stern authoritarian who nevertheless behaved in a logical manner in trying to uphold Roman rule. This is not at all the Pilate of the Gospels. Here was a man who showed weakness in the face of Jewish aggression. He gives in to their demands for the death of Jesus even though he himself could find no grounds for execution.

There are a number of things that could be going on here. The Gospel narrative may be deliberately blackening the Jews and excusing the actions of the Romans. Or Pilate may have rationally judged that his main aim was order; the Jews threatened disorder if they did not get what they wanted and so he should simply accede. Or, perhaps most plausibly, he was a man somewhat out of his depth. The intricacies of Jewish ideological in-fighting, of which Jesus was an element, are likely to have been somewhat opaque to an outsider. The One God of the Jews was a matter of perplexity for Romans. Pilate surely appreciated that pretenders to being 'King of the Jews' were a potential threat to order. But he cannot have quite understood why someone as patently pacifist and seemingly harmless as Jesus should have posed such a problem for the Jewish authorities.

1   *Fragments of late antique bronze head, Museo delle Terme, Rome. Evidence from the ancient world is almost always fragmentary*

His solution, famously, was to 'wash his hands' of the issue:

> When Pilate saw that he was getting nowhere, but that instead an uproar was starting, he took water and washed his hands in front of the crowd. 'I am innocent of this man's blood,' he said. 'It is your responsibility!' (Matthew 27.24)

This was a deliberate and ritual act making it clear that the moral responsibility was removed from him. From Pilate's perspective he was able, through debate and ritual, successfully to negotiate an obscure and difficult situation. But to view Pilate in this way is seeing through a glass darkly, a matter of guesswork. Pilate, as we know him, is a bit player in a tremendous myth, not so much in the sense of a falsehood as a peculiarly resonant narrative. Pilate's actions were necessary so that Christ could become a sacrifice as understood by his followers. We do not have to follow certain later traditions that suggested that Pilate and his wife afterwards converted to Christianity: his actions are comprehensible when seen from the point of view of a stressed military administrator.

The focus of the Gospels, of course, is on Christ. According to the New Testament narratives, at the moment when Jesus died the sky became black. There was a drum roll of thunder and the curtain of the Jewish Temple was torn in two. At the time, for the Roman authorities, the death of Christ was the occasion of nothing more than a spot of bad weather fomented by a dyspeptic sky god who sent raindrops to stream down the faces of the watching soldiers. The plain fact about the Crucifixion is that it was just another crucifixion. At the time it was really rather unremarkable, a fact which tells us a great deal about the ancient world. What sort of age was it where a man could, as a matter of ordinary justice, be nailed through the wrists and ankles onto a timber cross and left to die of suffocation and exposure? Where breaking the legs of the condemned was an act of mercy since it made for a speeder demise? Was this an age, perhaps, of special sadism and cruelty? An age in need of Christ?

Having seen the atrocities of the twentieth century, it is difficult to be harsh in the face of the low-technology violence of earlier centuries. After all, the clap of thunder which greeted the passing of Christ's spirit can scarcely have been as deafening as the sound of the dozens of nuclear weapons which have been tested, or of the two dropped in anger. It is the calculated personalisation of ancient brutality which strikes so emotive a human chord. This mode of killing was an act of torture and execution all in one. Moreover, the practice of crucifixion was also intended as bodily and mental desecration, since it represented the disfiguring and displaying of the body of the 'guilty'. It was intended as the ultimate insult and dishonour.

This was exactly how the person in Rome thought who, around 200, scrawled a graffito in plaster of a crucified donkey, with 'Alexamenos is worshipping his god' written underneath it. And though the Crucifixion was the chief glory of the Church, through the early Christian centuries the shame of the cross remained. For crucifixion was used as the method of execution for common criminals, pirates and slaves, as the presence of the thieves at the side of Christ attests. The cities of the ancient world were lined with the dead, in the form of funerary monuments, and the dying, in the shape of those undergoing such drawn-out executions. The shame of crucifixion meant that it was very rarely depicted in Christian art during the Roman period. It was only later, when the original banality of the act had been forgotten, that the crucifixion became something specific to Christ and to the enormity of the world's suffering which, in Christian understanding, he took upon himself.

Here we have a further problem, much like that with Pilate. Are we considering what Christ really was and did – or simply what believers and unbelievers said he was or did? The question, in fact, is easily answered. We only have 'Christ the image', in other words the way in which he was seen and interpreted by others. Therefore, it does not presently make sense to ask whether Christ was the son of God or not. The key question is what he was believed to have been and why this was so.

We have the words of Christ as extensively reported in the gospels. The same goes for Roman emperors whose deeds and *bons mots* were necessarily a matter of concern for the Roman elite with whom their destinies were intertwined. Only very rarely do we have their own words. For the most part what we see is the propaganda of the imperial house, or the snide remarks of opponents. There are occasional, rare, exceptions. Perhaps the most notable are the *Meditations* of Marcus Aurelius and the idiosyncratic selection of texts left by the fourth-century emperor Julian the Apostate. In the main we are dealing with stylised images. And since the vast majority of people in the ancient world heard about Jesus or the emperors through the testimony of others, the image was, for them, the reality.

This book, therefore, is a study of images, of the ways in which power was displayed and contested. It explores the fascinating way in which the pomp, violence and magnificent authoritarianism of Rome confronted, attacked and finally fused with the very distinct imagery and traditions of the reforming branch of Judaism that we know as Christianity. The result contributed powerfully to the transformation of the ancient world. But beyond that, the clash and union of Rome and Christianity was one of the most important processes in the history of the West. Had it not taken place our world would have been very different, perhaps unimaginably so.

Part 1

Here the history of Romans and Christians from the first to the fourth centuries AD is examined. Christianity was originally a minor feature of the life of the eastern provinces. It was strongly associated with anti-materialism and spiritual perfection. Status for the government and elites of the Roman Empire was to be found in grand displays of wealth, art and architecture. As Christianity began to spread it increasingly came into conflict with the State and its imperial ruler cult which Christians found an abomination. A series of imperial persecutions resulted in the popular adulation of the resulting martyrs. Finally, in the fourth century, emperor Constantine I converted to Christianity. He initiated a period in which the Church became integrated into the governing structures of the empire and was celebrated using the full range of ancient architectural and artistic magnificence.

2 A world of many beliefs

At the end of the fourth century, a hall off a colonnaded piazza was being constructed in Ostia, the port of Rome. The splendid decoration was executed using intricately cut stones of bright colours in the technique known as *opus sectile*. The upper walls were adorned with scenes including lions sinking their teeth into the flesh of deer. Below, a haloed bust of a figure giving a gesture of benediction could have been either Christ or a pagan holy man. At the end of the chamber was a raised area from which diners could watch entertainments in the room below. The decoration here similarly employed slabs of expensive stones such as porphyry, the colour of which acted as a symbol of imperial power during late antiquity. These luxurious and prestigious materials were being used to imitate the *opus mixtum* form of masonry which had been employed under the early empire. This featured bands of brickwork separating herring-bone panels of brick *opus reticulatum*. Each 'brick' of the fourth-century stone veneer was surrounded by thin strips of limestone representing mortar. Dunbabin has commented that 'simple though this decoration was, its preparation nevertheless required a phenomenal amount of work'. Almost 31,000 blocks are preserved from the lower sections. The prestigious elements of this decorative scheme lay not only in its sheer expense of time and materials. To appreciate this work requires a sophisticated appreciation of Roman building techniques running back over several centuries. The decoration of the building at Ostia was never completed. It has been suggested that this may have been due to religious strife since, at the end of the fourth century, aristocratic pagans were making a last stand against imperially-sponsored Christianity. But, intriguingly, it could easily have been a Christian chamber. There is no definitive distinction that can be found in the style of decoration.

This book is a visual history, not an art history. The difference is important: the appearance of the wider man-made environment rather than artistic styles will be focused upon. The underlying question is 'what difference did the adoption of the spiritual values of Christianity make to the appearance of the ancient world?' And, following on from that, 'to what extent can this change be used to explain the difference between Roman and medieval art and architecture?' And further, following the views of Gibbon, 'to what extent did Christianity bring down the empire and its associated splendours?' The relationship between the display of wealth and the establishment and maintenance of power during a period of immense political turbulence in western Europe will be considered. The art and architecture of the Roman elite was not 'mere show'. Vast expenditure on display was not irrational. People do not spend money without reason. Nor was this simply all about social competition, but rather social positioning, since goods are used to locate our social self and transmit knowledge about who and what we are. Those who spent on display were attempting to send messages and gain something in return. What they were trying to say, whom they were trying to address, and how they were interpreted will all be investigated.

An important background concept is that social links help to ensure a person's security. Display of wealth was a way of claiming importance in the eyes of superiors who could provide patronage and of inferiors who should realise their client subservience. Such show is thus ultimately about social relations. However, the forms of display might vary enormously depending on the values of the society in question. That is why keeping an eye on the forms of aristocratic display is hugely important in deciphering changing cultural attitudes.

From palaces to temples and from jewellery to weapons, some of the most dramatic evidence for the transition from Roman to Christian Europe is a result of the desire of rich people to spend their wealth in ways which have proved lastingly visible. Rulers and aristocrats dominated society and used material culture to express their social and spiritual beliefs and aspirations. Under the empire, substantial wealth was employed in acquiring and displaying Graeco-Roman elite literary and material culture. With their statues and aphorisms from Virgil the upper classes sought to distinguish themselves from their inferiors by a style of culture and moral life whose most resonant message was that it could not be shared by ordinary people. By the time of post-Roman Germanic kingdoms the elites of north-west Europe were visually communicating in significantly different ways. They were still attempting to assert their superiority so as to ensure the safety of perceived impregnability, but the means they employed had changed.

The traditional reason given for this has been a change of personnel. Quite simply, the 'barbarians' had taken over and their culture replaced that which had gone before. Much of the historiography has been bedevilled by ethnic partisanship as well as by constant disagreement about the significance of the so-called 'fall of Rome' – a notion, incidentally, not invented by Gibbon since it was current from at least the early sixth century in Byzantium. Gibbon, however, was as guilty as many of his contemporaries of a maudlin fascination with decay. He tells us that he first thought of writing the *Decline and Fall* when looking out across the ruins of the Roman forum, and his masterwork concludes with an overview of the physical decay of the city.

Gibbon has been stereotyped by the early twentieth-century historian Dill as telling the story of how 'the long tranquillity of the Roman sway ended in the violence and darkness of the Middle Age'. Yet Gibbon saw the empire's protracted collapse as partially its own fault. When his masterwork was complete, he wondered whether he should not have started earlier, placing the golden age of Rome not under the Antonines, but in the Republic, since he felt that the imperial system itself was inherently corrupt from the beginning. Such a view was shaped by Enlightenment horror at contemporary absolutist monarchy, as well as by the lurid tales of Suetonius which have forever tainted our views of the first emperors. Rome was a tyranny, which courted destruction through its repression of freedom. 'Barbarians' initially possessed greater vigour and liberty, although they were fatally marked by ignorance. The anti-materialist Church, as he perceived it, drew attention away from the physical world, many of the greatest man-made structures of which were neglected, then decayed and finally collapsed. In his analysis, the emperors and the Church were twin worms in the bud of imperial greatness and their mating at the end of antiquity was to produce lethal progeny. The empire was, in this analysis, sick from the beginning, since both Christianity and the imperial system itself were born in the age of Augustus and his successor Tiberius.

Barbarians from distant lands

Looking out over the imperial capital of Augustus at the time of Jesus' birth the Jewish traditions of the east registered as a peculiar blip on the cultural horizon. Since Herodotus in the fifth century BC, classical scholars had grown accustomed to looking out from their cultural capitals and wondering at the strange, uncivilised, *barbarian* inhabitants of the borderlands. Far in the north, darkness and cold gripped a land from which savages spewed like rats, filthy and naked. Living on roots, it was held that, if necessary, they could spend days at a time under water with only their nostrils showing. In those distant realms the very laws of nature seemed to be suspended. Seasons alternated between intense gloom and unremitting light. Frosts and mists clung to the land, whilst all round the northern seas heaved in strange motions and monsters ploughed through the depths of the oceans.

To the south, there was a terrible inverse: there the sun singed away the clouds leaving the deserts of the Sahara. Roman troops marching across those trackless wastes were equally prey to nomadic barbarian raids and to the attentions of the creatures of the sands. Lucan wrote an alarming description of the effects of African snakes' poisons. One venom could, supposedly, turn a body solid in seconds, another had the effect of liquefying the flesh such that it all soaked away into the ground leaving only the bones behind. Another would make the unfortunate corpse bloat and then explode. Another would leave the soldier shrieking in agony, only for his screams to be cut off as the wind blew away the dust into which his corpse had been reduced.

Herodotus, the first historian and anthropologist of Europe, has left us eloquent testimony of legends of one-eyed monsters and curiosities prowling the edges of the known world. In an even more lurid form such rumours would have been the standard fare of cautionary stories told to naughty children or of tales told by soldiers over too much wine in taverns. We might have expected intellectuals to know better, but they could not resist the lure of repeating anecdotes of exotic horror, as when the geographer Strabo commented that the furthest realms of the British Isles were inhabited by monstrous peoples who slept with their mothers and sisters and practised cannibalism. Not, as Strabo admitted, that he had any evidence to confirm such stories.

In a sense it did not matter whether there was hard fact involved or not. The psychology of the classical world rested on, amongst other things, a 'them and us' notion of a division between civilisation and barbarism. Quite simply, the *other* was suspect and the butt of fear and humour. The logic of these bizarre peoples somehow being part of the 'natural order' was not really thought through. Perhaps the idea was that these distant lands were themselves somehow mutant and perverse, and their habitants were suited to the darkness, the cold, the heat, the incessant winds, or whatever terrible bane lay over those regions at the far limits of the world.

This mixture of hostility and indifference to whatever lay in the peripheral vision of the Romans gave way to a more reasoned set of prejudices once one retreated back to the imperial frontiers. Here lay a garrisoned zone where the wild peoples of the boundaries were kept in check by the forces of the Roman state. And behind the frontier zone itself lay fertile land which produced the wealth that paid the taxes keeping the whole operation going. This was where the real problems of cultural definition began. It was not so bad in the west, for there the main cultural competitor to Rome had been pounded into virtual oblivion: the long series of Punic Wars against Carthage had culminated in the razing of the capital of Rome's greatest rival in the west. The rebuilt city was culturally, as well as politically, dominated by Rome. Punic and the other native languages were forced from elite culture to become the speech of the disempowered peasantry. Much the same happened in Spain, Britain and Gaul, where Celtic was at a particular disadvantage because it had not been a literary language.

The Roman cultural self-confidence which triumphed in the west was under much greater pressure in the east. In order to understand this phenom-enon we have to go several centuries back in time. Seen from the perspective of the classical Greece of Herodotus and Thucydides, central Italy was less than a sideshow. It hardly registered in a panorama of the western Mediterranean dominated by Greek colonies engaged in a competitive struggle against Punic influence. And this is to leave aside the simple fact that the west in general was seen as a distraction from the key places, events and personalities of the Hellenic world itself. Thus, the great Sicilian expedition with which Athens hoped dramatically to extend its authority was condemned by Thucydides as a policy disaster from the start since it meant that the people had lost touch with their true priority which was to control Greece. The catastrophic failure of the expedition effectively marked the end of major Greek concern with controlling politics in the west. Henceforth, Greek colonies in the area were left to fend pretty much for themselves.

The plain fact was that, at the time (fifth century BC), Rome was little more than a village. Its famed republican constitution resulted from an obscure stage in the crumbling of Etruscan control over central and northern Italy. The Etruscans, a mysterious people who seemed to have established a loose-knit alliance of kingships, saw their power overthrown by various local aristocratic coups, such as the one in which the Etruscan dynasty of Rome was expelled in favour of a clique of local Roman landowners. The ruthless militarism of the social system which grew up over the ensuing centuries was the generator of Roman imperial greatness. But by the time Rome had grown to the stature which allowed it to defeat Carthage, the eastern Mediterranean had been host to a range of powerful and impressive civilisations. The Near East, after all, has been regarded as one of the cradles of world civilisation. The greatest periods of Crete and Egypt long pre-dated classical Greece, which itself had built up 500 years of cultural achievement before being annexed by Rome. Greece, also presented a peculiar challenge to the Romans because their own culture was, to a substantial extent, derived from Hellenism. The Greeks were thus simultaneously 'us' and 'them'.

No such difficult and dangerous ambivalence surrounded the people of Israel. They were an anomaly even amongst the diverse and complex peoples of the ancient world. Yet if the Jews, with their strident monotheism, were hard for the pagan Romans to understand, our problem is somewhat different. Modern society, at least in Britain, is largely secular. This means that many of us have something of a problem in getting to grips with the one-time power and significance of ancient religions, especially those outside the broad Judaeo-Christian tradition.

When first studying Christianity I had the opportunity to live in Italy. Walking around Rome, the physical presence of religion immediately impressed me. There were churches everywhere. Not only that but there were also the mutilated remains of pagan temples. How is it possible to grasp what happened in pagan cults which have long been extinct? This is made even harder by the victory of Christ. Christians destroyed the pagan cults, including most of their texts and artefacts. We have to rely on Christian representations of what went on, and these display the Christian attitude that pagan gods were devils. A rather interesting parallel to this is suggested by Sabine MacCormack's book, *Religion in the Andes*. This examines the Christian conceptions of Inca religion in the newly conquered Peru of the sixteenth and seventeenth centuries. There repression was tempered by elements of curiosity and understanding, ranging from compassion for ignorance, to hatred at perceived evil in the ancient native beliefs. Understanding classical paganism will, inevitably, involve an element of conjecture.

Cults and philosophies

What, then, do we think we understand about classical paganism? It is perhaps best to consider it as a set of ritual and ideological systems, not really a system- atic 'religion', but more a series of interlocking cults. Originally, paganism appears to have been strongly animistic, preoccupied with spirits free in the world, in its water, wood, trees and so forth. Certain locations across the landscape were held to be especially sacred, particularly groves, caves and other places with legends attached to them. Shrines and temples with attendant priests, rites and endowments might grow up at such places, whilst further temples would be positioned in growing settlements or perhaps in country houses. The classical period was an age of many cults. Some deities had specific spheres of operation. For example, Mars was the god of war, whilst Venus was associated with fertility. Each promised access to and protec- tion or help from the supernatural, in return for various forms of devotion. Certain cults catered to particular human needs. That of Asclepius, for instance, was especially associated with healing illness. Although individuals might pray to a variety of gods and goddesses, many cults and deities were in competition with one another for attention.

It is necessary to forget the main religious heritage we have in the west, which is Christian, and thus forget about the importance of sin, of an afterlife, heaven and hell, and so forth. The main thing in ancient paganism was the here and now, or rather, the there and then. Gods manifested themselves in the world and they could do you good or do you evil. Sacrifices established polite relations with the divine realm whilst knowledge was sought by means of astrology, watching the stars and harnessing the services of auspices, harus- pices (who poked through the entrails of sacrificed beasts) and oracles. There was understood to be a reciprocal arrangement between the spiritual world and the physical: in other words if you pay respect to the gods they will help you and vice versa. By 'help' is meant aid in your day-to-day life, with the growth of crops and so forth, whilst by 'paying respect' is meant worship, which was primarily done through ritual acts of prayer and sacrifice. This could be in the form of ceremonial offerings to the gods, such as incense burnt on an altar or animals ritually slaughtered.

When thinking about the ancient world, it can be useful to refer briefly to modern India. The stereotypical images of the Indian subcontinent conjure up a world of bright colours, spices, swirling draped clothes, teeming cities, peasants, closely bound social ranks, temples, incense, splendour and poverty. This is not a description of the diverse reality of the modern subcontinent. It is a set of abstractions, yet it is one that could also be applied to the Roman Empire. Rome, before the age of the conversion to Christianity, had been a pagan society dominated by cult practice and philosophical beliefs which, if they find an echo in the modern world, find it in Hinduism and Buddhism. Hinduism provides a parallel for classical temples, statues, legends and incense.

2   *A rare standing example of a classical Roman temple, Maison Carrée, Nîmes.*
Leo Curran, Maecenas Archive

Buddhism echoes the world of ancient philosophy, which was a series of belief systems often dislocated from pagan cult practices and which sought to explain the nature of the universe and the correct way for humans to behave in it. Philosophy was mostly the leisure interest of educated and rich men, who might choose between morally serious Stoic, quasi-scientific Epicurean, world-challenging Cynic or other schools.

Where did pagan worship take place? There were household shrines. Each head of household was responsible for the worship of domestic gods. A platform and statue for such a shrine have been found at Silchester, for instance. But the main locus of holy ceremonial was in public temples, or, to be more precise, in temple complexes. The temple itself was a building designed to house the statue of the god in question. Moreover, statues were often understood to be animated in the ancient world: in other words, the god really did inhabit the statue in some sense. Temples were usually small inside, even the Parthenon, the bulk of which was made up of the colonnade all round the outside. That style of temple was very rare in the north-west of the empire. Most examples there were much less grand affairs looking more like small houses without those characteristic columns. In Italy, a typical temple had columns at the front only, placed at the top of a steep flight of steps. Similar designs were occasionally employed in the north-western provinces, for example at Nîmes. Around the temple proper – of whatever form — was a sacred area. It was here that the main ceremonies and sacrifices took place, together with ritual actions, libations, singing and chanting.

Some sites show the development of specific religious complexes. Perhaps one of the best British examples is at Lydney where a temple, large by Romano-British standards but still about the size of a small medieval parish church, was set in a large courtyard. To the north and east of the court were a long range of offices or guest rooms, a large courtyard building, and a separate baths complex. Celtic deities at sites such as this were frequently 'conflated' with Roman ones, that is local deities were represented in Roman guise, much as Jupiter was identified with Greek Zeus, a good example of this being the temple and healing cult of (Celtic) Sulis (Roman) Minerva at Bath.

Religious life was a colourful realm of activity that extended all through the classical city. There were of course rural cults but many major cults were explicitly woven into the life of local urban centres. The cult of Artemis at Ephesus was the cult of Ephesian Artemis, much as many medieval saints, for example Martin of Tours, were associated with particular churches in particular towns. Cult temples were often placed overlooking the Latin forum or Greek agora which was also the centre of trade and local government. This phenomenon of public religion has been referred to as 'civic cult'. The public nature of such worship is further illustrated by the fact that priests were not a separate caste in the main and such offices were often held alongside the performance of city magistracies.

Civic worship was carried out both for the good of the cities in which it was taking place and also on an individual basis as a result of personal needs and the expression of personal faith. One of the archaeologically visible expressions of this is provided by gifts to the gods (votives). Pliny described a lake in rural Italy of the second century which was surrounded by various temples, through the clear waters of which coins could be seen shining on the bottom. These were offerings to the gods thrown in by local people. Such practices are directly paralleled in the Romano-Celtic religions of Britain. At the fort at Carrawburgh near Hadrian's Wall there was a shrine of the goddess Coventina. It was a very simple and small temple, but the *cella* or central chamber covered a well. In this were found 13,000 Roman coins, together with pots, altars and incense burners which have provided dates down to the mid-fourth century.

People asked for help and they also accused. A mass of lead curse tablets have emerged from the sacred hot spring at Bath as well as from a number of temples across Britain. An example from Lydney reads as follows: 'to the divine Nodens. Silvianus has lost his ring and given half its worth to Nodens. Among those who bear the name Senecianus, let none enjoy health until he brings it back to Nodens.' Or there is the revolting curse from Clothall near Baldock: 'Tacita is cursed by this and declared putrefied like rotting blood.'

A single person might worship many gods. For a start there were the gods of the home and hearth, then there were the temples of the civic cults mentioned above, then there were various exotic cults, such as that of Isis from Egypt. There were cults of earthly rulers including the Roman emperors and there were what are often referred to as the eastern mystery cults, which offered personal salvation within an initiatory context of worship, two main examples of which are Mithraism and Christianity. The power of personal rather than public religious assistance can be seen as one factor in the rise of these belief systems. It is easy to stress the division between civic forms of worship associated with local government and the welfare of the State, and the 'oriental' ascetic/ordeal cults which offered personal revelation in return for adherence to codes of behaviour beyond that of the performance of particular rituals. This dichotomy is useful to bear in mind, but in fact each cult balanced ritual action with personal belief. The mysteries were originally part of the ancient spectrum of religious practice which encompassed the archaic Greek cult of Eleusis and its secret fertility initiations, and the religious hysteria of the priests of Cybele.

Yet Christianity, like the Judaism from which it emerged, was distinctive in many ways. The monotheism of the Jews was a matter of widespread incomprehension in the ancient world. The diversity of life was generally not thought to be explainable by the actions of a single deity. The crucial idea of the Israelites as God's chosen people was a matter of perplexity for outsiders. It was also an important political issue because the Israelites held their piety to be the basis for divine intervention which would free them from their oppressors. Deliverance for Israel would come through the agency of a prince of the line of David, king of Israel in the tenth century BC.

The main Jewish groups at the time of Jesus were the Sadducees, the Pharisees and Zealots. The Sadducees were supporters of traditional aristocratic rule. Pharisees were mainly concerned with textual criticism and the correct interpretation of Mosaic Law. The Zealots wished for violent revolt against Rome. Jesus, who if he was not seen as the son of God, the new David, was most obviously to be regarded as a prophet, combined new insights with Pharisaic analysis of correct behaviour. His humble origins marked him out as an object of scorn for the Sadducees. His radical interpretations marked him out as dangerous in the minds of most Pharisees. The Zealots, meanwhile, would have had no time for his pacifism. It is no wonder that there were many influential Jews who wanted him removed. But we need, for our current purposes, to distinguish Christ from Christianity, that initially very small sect of believers in his divinity. To begin with they faced incomprehension and hostility from the Jewish communities from which they had sprung. It is hardly surprising that the Roman governors and soldiery had problems understanding this new faith.

3 Via Sacra Nova in front of the Basilica Aemilia, Forum Romanum, at the heart of the empire

Unlike most of the diverse cults of the ancient world, Christianity, deriving as it did from Judaism, was not built for ideological co-existence. It was exclusive: the religion of the jealous god. Worship of the Christian God was held to be incompatible with any other form of religiosity. And even more outrageous to classical opinion was the Christian belief that all other deities were demons intent on leading mankind from the true spiritual and moral path. Jesus the condemned criminal was, for the average Roman of the first century, a bizarre focus for an incomprehensible cult. He was mentally joined with the one-eyed monsters as a freak of nature.

Yet freaks were far from unfamiliar, at least on the stinking and packed streets of the imperial capital where, as Tacitus said, 'all degraded and shameful practices collect and flourish'. It is crucial to realise that the ancient world was culturally extraordinarily diverse. Rome itself was a city of up to a million people many of whom were immigrants from across the empire and perhaps even beyond. The grand imperial inscriptions and titles liked to make procession of the wide sway of the capital and the varied peoples under its thumb. Parthians, Britons, Armenians, Syrians, Hispanics, Germans, Egyptians, and scores of others lived not only in their native lands, but also in the squares, homes and slave markets of the city of Rome. And whilst the Roman aristocracy affected an effortless superiority over such provincials and barbarians,

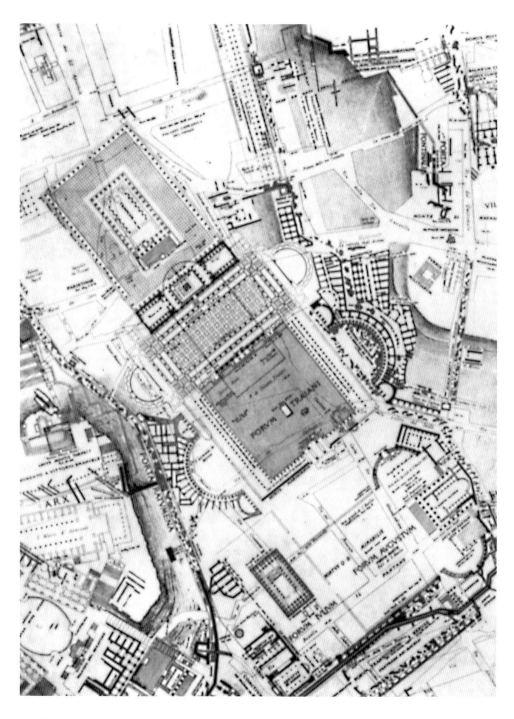

4   *Plan of the Imperial Fora, Rome*

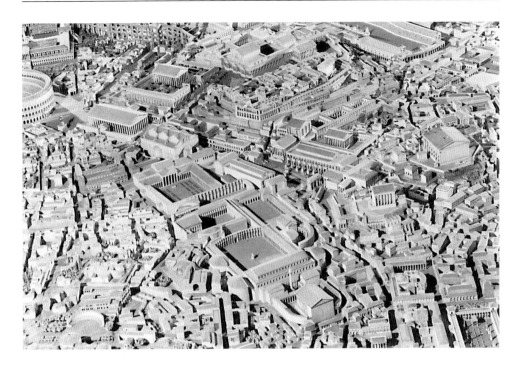

5   *Model of the Imperial Fora.* Mus. della Civilità Romana

they themselves were busy learning Greek and indulging tastes for exotic imports from across the then known world.

Christianity, for all its peculiarities, was a product of the Roman world, or at least of a region of the world ruled from Rome. It was a religious reform movement which emerged during a time of intense troubles for Jews within the empire. During the course of the first and second centuries Jewish political revolution was crushed by Roman military might, whereas Christian teachings came to be adopted where the ancestral religion had failed. This book is not an in-depth examination of theological issues. It is about the view from the centre, from Rome, and the way official opinion changed from indifference to puzzlement, disquiet, anger, acceptance and finally defence of Christianity. This story of changing attitudes will be illustrated by images of the physical world of ancient Rome and Christianity, which enable us to see not just how attitudes toward religion changed, but also how Christianity evolved and was eventually absorbed by the Roman establishment. In the end a compromise was struck whereby, very broadly and not always comfortably, the public arena was left in the hands of the government, whilst private life passed into the control of the Church. Thus souls could be saved along with the empire.

The physical magnificence of the Roman world will be considered first, then official attitudes as they evolved from indifference to persecution. Next the book looks at Christian acceptance of death and suffering, at the reasons for the failure of the persecutions, at Constantine and at the churches of the newly Christian empire (which provide a vivid illustration of the way in which the two cultural traditions came to merge). Finally, the end of empire and the survival of the Church will be examined.

Visual and spiritual

Recent years have seen the rise of minimalism in art and decoration. The adage 'less is more' has risen to prominence. This is a reflection of a rich and bloated developed world, where being thin is a greater achievement than being fat. Abundance, in food, as in decor, has become cheap. Refinement can often be more sharply displayed by refusing obvious ostentation. It is against this back-ground that the tastes of the elites of past centuries can seem as overstuffed as their furniture and waistcoats. This is true of the Victorian salon with its riot of knick-knacks, potted palms, prints, and elaborate wallpaper and it was also true of what was the acme of taste in the ancient world.

Roman buildings, and not simply the houses of the very rich, were to the modern eye heavily and perhaps excessively decorated. Available surfaces were painted, carved, moulded and embellished to provide a rich mixture of geometric and figural effects. Artists may have been anonymous and poorly regarded craftsmen, but their services were in considerable demand. It is likely that most reasonably sized towns would have supported a number of workshops. Of course, we rarely have good examples of paintings on board, or of textiles (the exceptions being those preserved from burials in the dry and drying sands of Egypt and the Near East), but we can tell from Pompeii and Herculaneum, where the similarly preserving layers of volcanic ash have left many decorations intact, that the walls of the houses of respectable citizens were bright with painted panels, trellises and architectural and vegetal fantasies.

The palaces of ancient times were similar to large houses, but distinguished by scale, grandeur, sophistication of execution and design and by the use of expensive materials. For instance, the Golden House (*Domus Aurea*) of Nero, in Rome, was reputedly decorated with gold and precious stones, a claim that might be imagined as carping social criticism, had we not the surviving evidence of gilded stucco mouldings at such sites as the Villa of the Caecilii at Tusculum which dates from the Hadrianic era. Such splendours were echoed in the personal possessions of the rich. These were displayed in ritual contexts such as banquets during which social rivalry could be played out through the conspicuous display of wealth in the form of astonishing foods, elaborate silverware and exotic retinues.

This ostentation was regarded as being a natural part of the rich abundance that the world could bestow if the gods were benevolent. Contemporary attention centred on the cult statue which was often encrusted with precious substances. Alternatively, plain terracotta, or wood of ancient holiness, was displayed in a splendid glistening setting, in a similar manner to the bones of martyrs in a Christian church. The treasure-context acted to identify as precious what did not look precious (an old statue or old bones). The very decoration schemes of many temples may have mirrored those of later churches, as appears to have been the case with the mosaic-embellished Lupercal Chapel discovered in Rome in the seventeenth century. Statues, reliefs and temple walls were painted. Prominent examples of scenes survive from all the great centres: Rome, Carthage, Athens, and so forth. The sacred enclosures, through frescoes, friezes, sculpture and statues, performed the act of

> drawing the eye with a very rich display of colour throughout . . . rewarding it with scenes and symbols full of meaning for even a stranger . . . they constituted the best means by which priests and pious alike could impress their beliefs on the public entering the shrines. (MacMullen, *Paganism in the Roman Empire*)

Many pagan temples became enormously wealthy through gifts and dedications. Augustus proclaimed in his *Res Gestae* (a boast to the populace of Rome) that he had removed 80 silver statues of himself from the streets and had, for their donors' sake, sent gifts of gold to the Temple of Apollo. But religious ostentation did not stop there – it spilled out onto the streets of the city. The study of C. Vibius Salutaris' will by Guy Rogers provides a fascinating insight into the workings of such public piety under the Empire. In 104 Salutaris, a leading citizen of Ephesus, left large sums of money for distributions, metal statues and for an organised procession. The main capital sum was deposited as an endowment of the Ephesian Artemis. The gold and silver images weighed 124lb. They were explicitly referred to as sacred.

Gilded statues sat in gilded sanctuaries upon gilded thrones. Christian monuments and their associated precious artefacts have been preserved by virtue of their continuing status as sacred. No such thing was true for the material culture of the pagan cults. Much marble statuary has survived, but precious metal could easily be melted down and reworked. Evidence for pagan treasure items is, therefore, scarce, but it does exist. A mid-third-century fresco in the synagogue of Dura Europus shows the Ark of the Covenant taken into the Philistine temple of Dagron. The statue is shown broken, whilst sacred utensils, bowls, pitchers and ladles, like those found from Byzantine village church treasures, lie scattered all over the floor, even though Scripture only refers to the crumbling of the cult statue.

Rituals are formal and repeatable behaviours which have the aim of regulating, presenting and explaining social relations. They can act to fix or reinforce ideas and so to protect against the shifting of meanings. Visual aspects to rituals can enhance their effectiveness by focusing the attention of the participants and viewers. This is particularly the case where expensive materials are employed. Therefore, the more expensive the trappings, the more important the ritual and its purposes may be assumed to be. The more impressive the cultic buildings and insignia, the more likely they were to stand out. Making the wealth of a cult visible also placed on display the potency of the divinity in question.

But at the same time such display coexisted with the idea that the immaterial and supernatural were superior to the material. Personal expression of this belief was made by many self-proclaimed 'philosophers', particularly those of the Cynic persuasion, and 'holy men', who protested their unconcern for the things of this world. A mosaic at Pompeii shows a builder's level. On one end are a wooden crook and food pouch (the attributes of the Cynic philosopher). On the other end are a sceptre, a piece of purple cloth and the white strip that was the Hellenistic diadem (the attributes of royalty). The level was in balance. Any cult that could entice people through splendour and yet find a convincing excuse for that very ostentation would be ideally positioned for influence. The spiritual and physical worlds were held by pagans to co-exist and intersect. Spiritual forces were present through the material world, albeit being concentrated at particular times and places. This is effectively what a temple or shrine was, a vessel in which to concentrate the sacred. By the making of offerings and prayers the deity was encouraged to take up residence and to listen to the questions and requests of the worshippers.

Of course, some temples were positioned in places which were already rich with spiritual power, as in the seemingly miraculous hot springs of the temple complex at Bath. Go to the city today and you can descend via the modern bath entrance to the main bathing pool of the Roman shrine. The visitor is given a 'wand', a dark phone-like object which provides a nasal running commentary without the inconvenience of having to pace round behind a human guide. The listener is thereby provided with the benefits of a modern scientific explanation. Water falls on nearby hills and penetrates into the soil and thence through a curving stratum of pervious bedrock which lies between impermeable layers. The water percolates downward, coming under increasing pressure and slowly heating up. In due course the warm water is forced up out of the other end of the aquifer resulting in a hot spring.

Now, we have no way of knowing that this is really what is happening. We simply have to trust the modern experts. The same thing can be said of the visitors in antiquity listening to the explanations of priests on the connection between spiritual presence and physical miracle. Even before the Romans arrived in the area, the native Celtic people had honoured the spring as the place of a water deity. The fact is that such hot water was out of the normal range of experience and, as such, it was put down to the mysterious action of divinity. This reasoning was followed by the Roman invaders, who established a temple and baths complex dedicated to a composite of the native deity and one of their own, the above-mentioned Sulis Minerva. At Bath, therefore, there was a literal hot-spot of divinity which only needed enhancing and channelling through artifice; this returns us to the connections between the material and the spiritual realms. On the one hand the spiritual realm only made itself prominently felt when it had physical forms, as in the miracles of Jesus. On the other hand people sought to focus the spiritual realm through physical construction of temples, shrines and altars.

Colour and brilliance were key aspects of grand classical architecture which could also be seen as gifts from the divine realm. Light was an important element in ancient spirituality. It streamed down from the heavens. Stars were often understood by Stoic philosophers as being souls of the deceased glimmering in the sky. It was, therefore, a short step to think in terms of solar cults. Jupiter, the chief Roman deity, was a sky god. The identification of the sky with divinity became more explicit over time with the rise of the cult of the divine sun, Sol Invictus, which was particularly favoured by third-century emperors.

Light could be seen and used as a metaphor for goodness in opposition to the idea of darkness, blackness, night and evil. The fact that we share something of the same set of cultural oppositions with the Romans does not mean that every culture does so, but nevertheless the fear of the dark may have some basic biological imperative in that the eye is the premier human organ of sense, something attested to by the richness and complexity of our perception of colour which is lacking in many other animals. Light could be seen as a life force, such that those in love, and perhaps on the verge of procreating, were said to burn brightly. Moreover, the soul itself was held to shine, greater souls shining more than lesser ones. This is the origin of the nimbus, with which we are most familiar in depictions of saints. But this was originally an ancient attribute showing the spiritual greatness shining forth from the heads of great leaders, gods and heroes.

Jesus said of himself, 'I am the light of the world; he who follows me will not walk in darkness' (John 8: 12). This tendency to think in terms of light and goodness, was, if anything, to become more pronounced as antiquity progressed. It was a strong element in the Christian traditions which were themselves influenced by schools of pagan thought that were rising in popularity during the later Roman Empire. Above all, the school of Neo-Platonic philosophy emphasised the connection between physical and spiritual realms, with matter being the first stage in contemplating divinity. Light functioned as an immaterial state of matter which was in a halfway stage between the two states. The physical was, in such understanding, not in opposition to the spiritual, but in intimate and significant connection with it.

Emperors, power and display

Since there was no fixed boundary between the physical and the spiritual realms there was no clear division between the gods and humans in much pagan thought. Divinities could be seen in terms of the *scale* of their potency. They had souls of transcendent power. The souls of ordinary people could be a seen as simply being like those of deities but on a very small scale. The power of great princes could itself be seen as a result of political, military and dynastic advantages. But, equally, it was assumed that the will of the gods must play a significant role. Kingdoms, and indeed the empire, depended ultimately on the goodwill of the supernatural realm, without which crops would not burgeon, women would die in childbirth and naval galleys would sink in storms at sea. This is what State religion was for in pagan Rome. Whilst individual piety would be directed towards personal needs, the leaders of a community were responsible for the good fortune of their city or state. To that end the public rituals of the city of Rome conducted by the emperor in his position as chief priest (*Pontifex Maximus*) such as that of Jupiter Best and Greatest (*Optimus Maximus*) were versions writ large of those carried out by local magistrates who were expected to lead communal rites in provincial city temples.

But if we consider the position of the emperor, we are faced with an enigma. How was it that a single man was able to have such an unprecedented degree of control over so many people? In order to make sense of this it was convenient to think in terms of divine sanction. Thus, Augustus, the first emperor, could be perceived as being peculiarly blessed by the gods. They must have singled him out for this purpose. And for that to be so Augustus must have some extraordinary connection with them. In fact the very enormity of Augustus' power made him a god-like figure, a fact communicated by the idealised images of the emperor which were placed in towns all across the provinces. The emperor was held to inhabit his image, much as a god inhabited his, such that grasping the robe of the statue was the equivalent of running to the emperor in person and pleading for imperial justice over the heads of the local authorities.

Greek cities had long been used to living under the thumb of absolute Hellenistic kings, a fact which the worship of such rulers served to render comprehensible. After all, identification of quasi-divinity meant that the citizens established a way of relating to the super-powerful imperial entity and of showing their respect and loyalty. The situation in Rome was a little more complex. On the one hand republican Rome, which came to an end with Augustus, had had a luxury-regulating anti-monarchic culture, based on the expulsion of the Etruscan monarchs *c.*500 BC. On the other, Rome increasingly celebrated its rise by the erection of grand buildings and ceremonials in the name of the city and of prominent senators. The ideology of the republic is best attested through the far from disinterested chroniclers of the period of its failure. The political system, by the time it is richly documented, that is the second and first centuries BC, was praised by the Greek Polybius as being the ideal, balanced constitution. It was supposedly balanced because it combined elements of the three main governing systems of ancient city states, monarchy (rule by one person), oligarchy (rule by an elite group) and democracy (rule by free adult males). The chief magistrates, the consuls, represented the first element, the aristocratic senate the second and the voting assemblies responsible for appointing the magistrates represented the third.

Victorious generals who were voted a 'triumph' were offered an occasion when they would appear as a god in the role once played by kings. The elite symbols, a purple cloak and gold ornaments, were taken from a sacred statue and worn by the state's hero, his face painted to look like terracotta, as he was drawn through the streets in a gilded chariot. But this quasi-divine status was temporary and entirely in the gift of the aristocratic peer group. Moreover, the general was constantly reminded 'remember, you are but a man'. This control and regulation was necessary because the power of rulers was expressed and claimed by elaborate ceremonial. A highly significant example of such an expression was the funeral, that occasion when the dangerous handover from one regime to another lent a political edge to the proceedings. Those with an interest in the succession could use the occasion to build their own reputation by the way in which the deceased was presented. A famous example of this was the funeral procession of Alexander the Great. The hearse itself took two years to build and took the form of an Ionic temple, roofed with gold, inside which Alexander's mummy was enclosed in a golden sarcophagus over which was draped his purple cloak. Golden nets prevented the profane gaze from falling on it and no fewer than 64 mules were needed to drag the hearse on its lengthy processional route.

In late republican Rome Julius Caesar was accused of aiming at monarchy and it was gossiped that he was about to assume the material trappings of kingship. His assassination prompted the caution of his successor Augustus in the area of self-promotion. The emperor was supposedly to be 'first among equals' in the senate. But the reality was revealed through the process of succession in the Julio-Claudian family. Rome was effectively in the hands of a royal dynasty. Whether through insanity, pride or simple confidence, the later Julio-Claudians were far more blatant than their predecessors. The behaviour and open display of power by Nero rubbed the noses of the senatorial elite in the fact of their own subservience. They, predictably, loathed him, but the ordinary people of Rome seem to have admired the imperial glamour. Flowers kept appearing at the deposed ruler's grave and rumours circulated for centuries that Nero was simply in hiding and would return one day to rule the empire.

In the long run the grand style of Nero was to become typical of the imperial office as, over time, the institution of the imperial monarchy was bolstered and surrounded by all manner of symbolism and self-promotion. This took direct forms, such as personal dress and palaces, or indirect ones, as coins and imperial images circulated across the Empire. The varied forms of official dress, coins, monuments and ceremonies reflected the myriad aspects of imperial pre-eminence. The reality of the immense imperial power demanded a suitably splendid material presentation for the office and its holder.

Why was this style employed? The battle was for the minds and hearts of potential adherents. It is hardly surprising that the senatorial nobility was initially reluctant to embrace the imperial version and vision of reality. The lower classes and provincial elites, particularly in Greece, may have been much more eager to make use of images and ritual so as to make sense of their subservience. Being powerless to break free, they seemed to have wished to share in the grandeur of the imperial house. The greatness and even the divinity of the victor made their subservience seem comprehensible and more honourable. In these circumstances there was a considerable Empire-wide movement to represent and understand the emperor, or at least his ancestors, as divine.

The human and divine spheres were linked by intermediaries such as heroes, or forces such as victory and fortune. Imperial divinity should be understood in the context of such interconnection. Augustus, in the wake of Caesar's assassination, wished to proceed with caution. But his successors, feeling themselves more secure, relaxed such controls. Imperial divinity became slowly more respected in Rome itself, even amongst the senatorial class. There was an element of political manipulation in this process but belief also played a considerable role. For, if emperors were not divine, the scale of their rule must have meant that they were, at the very least, especially blessed by the gods. Keith Hopkins has argued that it is too simple to conclude that the imperial cult was either profound or a sham. He concludes that there were greater and lesser degrees of respect on the part of individual aristocrats, philosophers and the populace at large. The ceremony of *damnatio memoriae*, when sacred images and inscriptions of an ex-emperor were destroyed, was the occasion for the gleeful exposure of an all too human fraud. Yet if good and bad emperors came and went, the notion of imperial divinity, if anything, strengthened in the first and second centuries.

'Treasures in heaven'

The ignominious treatment meted out to Christ was similarly intended to erase him from memory and so from having ongoing significance. The preservation of his words, or at least the myth of him as preserved in the Gospels, shows the failure of a Roman action based on a physical ceremony of degradation. His followers could soon read that he had preached that the ostentation of pagan and much of Jewish worship was wrong. The key text for this is Matthew 6, which also contains the Lord's Prayer ('Our Father who is in heaven, hallowed be your name . . . ') and so can hardly be regarded as a peripheral section of the Gospel. The message of the chapter is unambiguous:

Do not, as Jews and pagans did, make a public show of your piety:

Matthew 6.1: 'Beware of practising your piety before men in order to be seen by them; for then you will have no reward from your Father who is in heaven.'

And do not give charity in public in search of popular fame:

6.2: 'Thus, when you give alms, sound no trumpet before you, as the hypocrites do in the synagogues and in the streets, that they may be praised by men.'

Do not create an elaborate textual liturgy (use the Lord's Prayer instead):

6.7: 'And in praying do not heap up empty phrases as the Gentiles do; for they think that they will be heard for their many words.'

Do not hoard physical wealth:

6.19-20: 'Do not lay up for yourselves treasures on earth, where moth and rust consume and where thieves break in and steal, but lay up for yourselves treasures in heaven, where neither moth nor rust consumes and where thieves do not break in and steal.'
6.24: 'No one can serve two masters; for either he will hate the one and love the other, or he will be devoted to the one and despise the other. You cannot serve God and mammon.'

This section of the sayings of Jesus is not found in Mark and Luke, the other gospels which seem to share an origin in a text no longer extant which scholars call 'Q'. Nevertheless, the metaphor of treasure in heaven is found across these 'synoptic' gospels:

Matthew 19.21: 'Jesus said to him, "If you would be perfect, go, sell what you possess and give to the poor, and you will have treasure in heaven; and come, follow me."'
Mark 10.21: 'And Jesus looking upon him loved him, and said to him, "You lack one thing; go, sell what you have, and give to the poor, and you will have treasure in heaven; and come, follow me."'
Luke 18.22: 'And when Jesus heard it, he said to him, "One thing you still lack. Sell all that you have and distribute to the poor, and you will have treasure in heaven; and come, follow me."'

The problem with renouncing physicality is that, short of immediate suicide, it is not entirely possible. Long theological debates through the centuries centred on the extent to which Jesus did have his own possessions or whether the disciples held all goods in common. And further, whether goods held thus in common represent conformity with the call to sell wealth and give it to the poor. After all, if possessions are a bane, you are hardly doing a favour by giving them to others. The problem is that the facts of the Gospels do not appear to fit and perhaps cannot be fitted neatly with Jesus' assertions, which appear clear and dogmatic but which must have been meant as suggestions towards appropriate behaviour. This constant tension between ideals and reality and the complex special pleading made in order to justify compromise was to be a key factor throughout the history of Christianity as an organised, and often very wealthy, religion.

Jesus said, 'Why are you anxious about clothing? Consider the lilies of the field, how they grow; they neither toil nor spin; yet I tell you, even Solomon in all his glory was not arrayed like one of these' (Matthew 6.28–9). By so arguing, and yet being seen as King of the Jews, he was totally upsetting the notion of how a powerful ruler should appear. He was thus mocked by the Romans:

> Mark 15.16-20: 'And the soldiers led him away inside the palace; and they called together the whole battalion. And they clothed him in a purple cloak, and, plaiting a crown of thorns, they put it on him. And they began to salute him, "Hail, King of the Jews!" And they struck his head with a reed, and spat upon him, and they knelt down in homage to him. And when they had mocked him, they stripped him of the purple cloak, and put his own clothes back on him.'

The same story appears in John 19, Luke 23 and Matthew 27. The ideological and spiritual impotence of Jesus, as seen by the Romans, was demonstrated in a satirical version of royal ritual. The physical splendour of the ancient pagan world was contrasted with Jesus' miserable degradation. But this disjunction between splendid pagan and humble Christian was not to last. Christianity came to be so enmeshed in the governing and cultural structures of the ancient world that, arguably, it came to possess greater physical splendour than the state itself by the end of antiquity. It is not my purpose to decide whether this was a good or a bad thing. I want to understand how it was that, like the commandment 'thou shalt not kill', such words of Jesus came to be widely disregarded, or were understood, not literally, but as metaphors. This study explores the way in which the spirituality of Jesus came to be fused with the carnal Roman world that had mocked and destroyed him in the flesh.

3 The blood of the martyrs

Christianity can be seen, in its earliest forms, as a protest movement against the moral state of the people of Israel. They had strayed from the true path in their worldliness and pride. The only deliverance would come from living in accordance with the will of God. In the meantime, the gentiles had to be tolerated and, more radically, loved. One of Christ's messages was that you must continue to support the imperial regime by paying taxes ('render unto Caesar that which is Caesar's and render unto God that which is God's', Matthew 22.21). But crucial, and revolutionary, was his teaching that salvation was not the preserve of the people of Israel alone.

Matthew tells us that a centurion came to Jesus:

> Mathew 8.10-12: 'When Jesus heard him, he marvelled, and said to those who followed him, "Truly, I say to you, not even in Israel have I found such faith. I tell you, many will come from east and west and sit at table with Abraham, Isaac, and Jacob in the kingdom of heaven, while the sons of the kingdom will be thrown into the outer darkness; there men will weep and gnash their teeth."'

The *Acts of the Apostles* give testimony to the way in which the disciples took the message of Jesus to whomever would receive it. This was vital for the survival and spread of Christianity in the face of massive Jewish distrust or indifference. But it was the conversion of pagans that first marked out Christianity as a threat in the minds of Roman governors who believed that the vitality of the State depended on worship and appeasement of pagan deities. Nevertheless, it should be made clear that persecution of Christians was never carried out systematically by the Roman state until that under Decius in 250. The threat was simply not perceived as requiring systematic measures while Christians were such a tiny minority. Having said that, the strangeness of the cult of the crucified criminal quickly gave them a profile and notoriety greater than their numbers.

In July 64 a great fire broke out in Rome. Only four of the 14 districts of the city entirely escaped damage. Our later sources suggest that rumours swept the city that the emperor Nero was to blame. Certainly, Nero's great palace, the Golden House, emerged from a vast swathe of public land which was then turned over to the imperial pleasure after the fire, for the construction of vistas, villas and walkways. The whole thing could have seemed like an act of imperial land clearance. Whatever the case was, Nero, according to our unsympathetic sources, fastened the blame on

> a class hated for their abominations, called Christians by the populace. Christus, from whom the name had its origin, suffered the supreme penalty under the reign of Tiberius, at the hands of one of our procurators, Pontius Pilatus, and a deadly superstition, thus checked for a moment, again broke out not only in Judaea, the first course of the evil, but also in the city, where all things hideous and shameful from every part of the world swirl in and rise to popularity.

This writer is Tacitus, who was proconsul of the Roman province of Asia (which is now part of Turkey) from 112-3 and, as such, would have been familiar with Christians who seem to have been relatively numerous there.

> An arrest was made of all who confessed: then, on their informa-tion, an immense multitude was convicted, not so much for the crime of arson as of hatred of the human race. Mockery of every sort was added to their deaths. Covered with the skins of beasts, they were torn by dogs and perished, or were nailed to crosses, or were doomed to the flames. These served to illuminate the night when daylight failed. Nero had thrown open his gardens for the spectacle, and was exhibiting a show in the circus, while he mingled with the people in the dress of a charioteer or drove about in a chariot. Hence, even for criminals who deserved extreme and exemplary punishment, there arose compassion; for it was not, as it seemed, for the public good, but to one man's cruelty, that they were being killed.

Christians were clearly a known and despised minority. Tacitus was disgusted by them yet, in this narrative, they are a sideshow to his real concern, which is the abusive nature of imperial power under Nero. The methods of killing were not novel, but Nero staged the whole thing in his private gardens and rode about in a chariot, thereby distorting public justice into private entertainment. The element of mockery is surely a re-enactment of the original insult, Jesus' crucifixion. Yet, as with that killing, the results were paradoxical. What was meant to shame led to a degree of concern and perhaps, even, sympathy or admiration on the part of witnesses. According to Tacitus, the Christians' true crime was 'hatred of the human race' which was a charge also made against magicians, and for which the penalty was burning. Magic was illegitimate tampering with spiritual forces, which, like an amateur playing with a fuse box, could be very dangerous. Christians shared with Jews an apocalyptic tradition which looked forward to the destruction of impious worldly powers by supernatural means. Perhaps they showed joy at the material destruction of Rome, and so made themselves a target for popular prejudice and suspicion.

The sacred rites of the Christians were also a matter for gossip and scandal. The very fact that worship was carried out in closed communities of believers encouraged wild rumours as to what took place. Holy Communion, the ritual remembrance of Christ, through the re-enactment of his Last Supper, led to the most lurid misconceptions of this ceremony.

> Mark 14.22-4: 'And as they were eating, he took bread, and blessed, and broke it, and gave it to them, and said, "Take; this is my body." And he took a cup, and when he had given thanks he gave it to them, and they all drank of it. And he said to them, "This is my blood of the covenant, which is poured out for many."'

After 1 Corinthians 11.23-5 the first mention of the Eucharist comes in the *Didache*, an obscure, late first-century document which is probably from Syria. This discusses baptism, the thrice-daily recitation of the Lord's Prayer, and then describes the Eucharist: 'we thank thee, our Father, for the holy vine of David, thy son, whom you did make known to us through Jesus, thy son'.

This is my body . . . this is my blood . . . The Roman Catholic Church today holds to the doctrine of transubstantiation, whereby the bread and wine are literally transformed into the body and blood of Christ, rather than simply acting as symbols. The eating of sacrificial animals was central to pagan worship. The eating of the deity would, however, have seemed at best disgusting cannibalism, and at worst, grotesque blasphemy. This was a cult that worshipped a condemned criminal and then symbolically ate his body and drank his blood!

It is hardly surprising that Christianity did not lack for enemies in the community at large. But matters were made worse by the phenomenon of the enemy within. The *Didache* contains strong warnings against heretics: 'whomsoever then shall come and teach you all these things aforesaid, receive him. But if the teacher himself is perverse and teach another doctrine to destroy these things, hear him not . . . every prophet that teaches the truth if he does not do what he teaches is a false prophet . . . '

The problem was partly one of disorganisation. There was no such thing as the Church. There were churches, that is local groups of Christians. Believers wandered from city to city, spreading slightly different versions of the good news. Much of the variety stemmed from the way in which Christianity had emerged from Judaism, which was itself split into several strands of opinion. Moreover, Christianity was starting to spread through pagan communities. The key vehicle for its spread, as witnessed by the language of the New Testament, was Koine, 'street' as opposed to literary Greek. Once beyond Israel and the communities of the Diaspora after the disasters of the Jewish wars in the mid-first century, Christian proselytisers found themselves not only competing with the priests of pagan temples, but with adherents of the varied forms of classical philosophy. For Christianity, unlike paganism, combined ritual practices of worship with philosophical understandings of the universe and suitable behaviour and morals.

Christianity, therefore, faced alternative belief systems which continued to have considerable influence on the thinking of many converts from paganism. Justin was born *c.*100 in Nabulus in Palestine and martyred in Rome *c.*165. His writings represent a pioneering attempt to understand Christianity within the contexts and concepts of classical philosophy. He had studied a range of philosophical thought systems before becoming a Christian in 132. Soon afterwards he began the life of a wandering preacher, expounding his new beliefs, with the particular hope of converting educated pagans. He spent much time in Rome and it was as the result of his debate with the Cynic philosopher Crescens that he was denounced to the city prefect and subsequently condemned to death. Cynics were notorious for their denigration of worldly concerns and with this Justin, as a Christian, might have been expected to agree. Yet his attempts to justify such beliefs by comparing the lives and deaths of Christ and Socrates may have alienated people on both sides of the ideological divide.

> When Socrates endeavoured by true reason and examination to bring these things to light and deliver men from demons, then the demons themselves, by means of men who rejoiced in iniquity, caused his death as an atheist and profane person, on the charge that he was introducing new divinities; and today the demons act so to us Christians.

The larger cities of the second-century east clearly possessed a ferment of ideas and cultures. Temples, cults and holy men competed one against another for attention both from the divine realm and from passers-by. This world, peopled perhaps more by charlatans than visionaries, comes brilliantly to life in the satirical works of Lucian. His most savage portrait is of Alexander the False Prophet, who was pilloried by Christians and Epicureans, and who faked an entire cult based on the worship of a half-human, half-snake (in fact, a snake with a mask on). His satire on the life of Peregrinus is almost as extreme. This philosopher, a Cynic, killed himself on a funeral pyre in 165 at the close of the Olympic games. His stance was of lack of concern for the things of this world. The crucial difference compared with Christians was that were not supposed to seek martyrdom, only to accept it if God willed it. Lucian thought that the whole thing was a publicity stunt which got out of hand. Peregrinus thought, mistakenly, that the crowd would allow him to back out at the last minute, after he had gained his 15 minutes of fame and adulation.

It does not matter whether these people were stupid, mad, or divinely inspired. The important question is what people thought of them before and after their deaths. A further interesting point comes from the fact that Peregrinus was imprisoned for a while for temporarily converting, or pretending to convert, and he became a big name in the Christian community. Lucian accused him of doing this for mercenary reasons. There was, according to Lucian, plenty of money to be made from offerings from Christian visitors. They treated imprisoned Christians with compassion, both spiritual and financial. Lucian's judgement on the Christians was that they were people who were willing to believe anything: 'the poor wretches have convinced themselves, first and foremost, that they are going to be immortal, and live for all time, in consequence of which they despise death and even willingly give themselves into custody'.

Puzzlement and concern

What we are also looking at here is a connection between individual action and mob activity. It is quite clear that Christians banded together, just as their enemies joined to oppose them. It was this kind of behaviour, of individuals sparking general unrest, that was particularly likely to arouse the concerns of Roman governors, the main aim of whom was to keep the peace.

Pliny was sent as governor to Bithynia (now northern-central Turkey) in 112 by Trajan. He published his correspondence with the emperor: in other words, he circulated some of his letters for the purpose of demonstrating his fine style and high connections. These texts show that he was not sure what to do about the Christians. A number of them had been denounced to him. If they insisted on swearing allegiance to its tenets despite threats, he thought that they should be executed, but if Roman citizens, they were to be put aside to be sent to Rome. The very fact that trials were being held induced others to bring charges, and an unsigned accusatory list of names appeared. Pliny let go those who denied being Christian and who 'recited a prayer to the gods at my recitation, made supplication with incense and wine to your [Trajan's] statue, which I had brought into court for the purpose together with images of the gods, and who moreover cursed Christ'. Yet Pliny was perplexed, not simply by the behaviour of the people who would not recant but by the very nature of the cult itself. He questioned the accused at length.

> They maintained, however, that the amount of their fault or error had been this, that it was their habit on a fixed day to assemble before daylight and recite by turns a form of words to Christ as a god, and that they bound themselves with an oath, not for any criminal purpose, but that they would not commit theft or robbery or adultery, would not break their word, and not deny money when asked. After this was done it was their custom to depart and take food, but food of an ordinary and harmless kind.

Pliny had two serving maids tortured (who were known as 'deaconesses', he tells us) in order to test these assertions but found 'nothing more than perverse and extravagant superstition'. He then goes on to say that he adjourned the case and consulted the emperor, perhaps because important people were involved. He did this:

> . . . on account of the number of those in danger, for many of all ages and every rank, and also of both sexes are brought into present or future danger. The contagion of that superstition has penetrated not the cities only, but the villages and the countryside, yet it seems possible to stop it and put it right. At any rate it is certain enough that the almost deserted temples begin to be used once more . . .

The problem was not so much the spiritual fate of the individuals, but of society as a whole, if the main temples of the pagan gods were being neglected. The reference to the 'almost deserted temples' is very interesting. Reading this sort of language in the context of the Christianised empire of the fourth century it is easy to believe in a picture of abandonment and decay. At the time of Pliny, however, there is no archaeological evidence for this. What we are seeing here is hyperbole, a literary form which would develop steadily as religious conflict became considerably less rare over the course of the empire.

Trajan replied that anonymous denunciations were to be inadmissible, but that proven or self-acknowledged cases should be punished with death. To the modern mind a capital penalty might seem appropriate only for the most heinous offences, and some say it is never fully justified. However, execution was not a particularly remarkable occurrence in the ancient world. Anyone involved in the upper reaches of government knew that it was an occupational hazard of high office. Emperors could be, and were, deposed and disposed of. The majority of the servants of the State were soldiers who were trained to kill. And anyone opposing the State knew that they were opposing the greatest army of antiquity. The Christians were simply one more group amongst a range of deviants, miscreants and incompetents of many stripes who were sentenced to death by governors.

Prison was not highly developed in antiquity. Those found guilty were generally fined, banished, mutilated or executed. The main motivation behind such imperial justice was the maintenance of the political status quo in favour of the Romans. Anything that threatened to arouse local unrest was a potential target for retribution. It was in that context that Hadrian, in 125, wrote to the then proconsul of Asia, Caius Minucius Fundanus, saying that mob agitation should not automatically be given sway in cases against Christians. In other words, the key concern of the State was not religious persecution but local stability. Governors were encouraged to quieten the crowd using whatever means they thought fit, either setting the soldiery on them, persuading them that Christians were not a problem, or pressing ahead with execution. The attention of the State, therefore, was not primarily intent on enforcing religious conformity.

But we might well ask why there were mobs of people baying for the blood of Christians. Many Jews were hostile since they regarded Christians as heretics. Pagans might fear and distrust this strange new sect with its secret ceremonies. But beyond all this, and more to the point, Christianity was eroding certain aspects of traditional morality and family life. Wives were encouraged to spend time in church away from their pagan husbands. Even more seriously, daughters were encouraged to resist marriage, sex and childbirth.

The origins of the Christian tradition of sexual abstinence can be found in Old Testament purity taboos. And they have some connection with Christian ambiguity on the goodness or otherwise of the physical world. But it is clear that St Paul and his followers played a considerable role in pushing the radical espousal of virginity by Christian communities, as Peter Brown has documented in his important study, *The Body and Society*. Virginity was regarded as bizarre and unnatural by the pagan majority. They saw it as a perverse refusal to continue the family line which endangered property holdings. Many Christians, however, believed that the end of time was coming, the true family was the Church, and individuals were kept from sin by holding property in common for the good of all.

Imagine if a girl of 12, who had never left home before, was promised in dynastic marriage to a man she had never met and who was four times her age. Christians would counsel her to refuse to have sex with the man. The parents, on hearing that Christians were involved, were quite likely to be enraged and complain to the authorities, or form a lynch mob with other aggrieved families. Such persecution was not just at the hands of pagans or Jews within the context of imperial justice. Justin tells us that Barcochba, the leader of the last Jewish revolt against Rome in 132-5, ordered that Christians should be 'led to cruel punishments unless they would deny Jesus Christ.'

The key thing about those who died for their Christian belief was not simply that they were the object of fascination at the time, whether from admirers, from uncomprehending observers or from implacable enemies, but that their deeds were written down and transmitted. These martyrs were understood by Christian communities across the empire as being individuals whose actions paralleled those of Christ himself. This understanding was formed and developed through the texts that are now referred to as 'martyr acts' which describe these killings.

One of the earliest of the authentic acts appears in the form of a letter written at a disputed date in the mid-second century to the church of Philomelium in Asia Minor describing the death of Polycarp, bishop of nearby Smyrna. In the days before his arrest Polycarp moved about between farms outside the city, but was caught and did not resist arrest. The chief of police of the city, Herod, with his father Nicetes, tried to persuade Polycarp

6 *Bullfight, Amphitheatre, Arles. Bullfights are an echo of ancient violence.*
Copyright Leo Curran, Maecenas Archive

to recant as they rode together in the carriage that led them to the stadium. They then fell into a rage when he would not and they ordered the carriage to proceed into the stadium where he was brought before the local governor, the Roman proconsul of Asia.

The proconsul tried to persuade him to abandon his faith, urging, '"have respect for your old age" and the rest of it, according to the customary form. "Swear by the genius of Caesar, change your mind, say away with the atheists."'

Polycarp was threatened with beasts and fire. The crowds, Jews and pagans, screamed down that he should be thrown to a lion, but there was none available since the games were ended, so they called for him to be burnt. The mob got kindling together when the proconsul announced the sentence of execution. But Polycarp's body would not burn: 'The fire made the appearance of a vaulted roof, like a ship's sail filling out with the wind and it walled around the body of the martyr like a ring . . . Moreover, we caught a fragrance as of the breath of frankincense.' Since the fire was not hurting him, he was then stabbed by the executioner but so much blood poured out that the fire was extinguished.

At this he expired and the Jews then burnt the body. The Christians took the bones 'more valuable than precious stones and finer than gold, and lay them where they were fitting'. This happened, the letter tells us, 'that to us the Lord might once again give us an example of the martyrdom which resembles the gospel story'.

I will give two possible interpretations of these events which are not necessarily exclusively true or false. The first picture is of Polycarp as a man convinced that he was about to go to heaven. He did not seek martyrdom, but did not resist it when it came, since he believed this to be by the will of God. He did not see himself as being a parallel of Christ but, in not resisting arrest, was simply accepting the burden of reality that Christians were often called upon to suffer on this earth for their beliefs. He was a deeply sincere and brave man.

In the other interpretation Polycarp was deluded by the belief that he would most surely enter heaven through martyrdom. He was 86 and was not expecting to live much longer. The fact that he hid outside the town indicated that he was trying to avoid capture. He could not resist when he was found because of his old age. He was stubborn in refusing to change his views in order to save his skin. Moreover, he may have enjoyed the ongoing adulation of his Christian followers. Furthermore, classical society was fascinated by the issue of remembrance of important people, as witnessed by the craze for grand funeral monuments and inscriptions on buildings which were intended as memorials to the builders. Polycarp's greatest concern, then, was for his personal glory during his lifetime and after his death. Of course, all of this conjecture rests on the surviving document which is intended as an act of praise for Polycarp, providing an exemplar for other potential martyrs. We, therefore, can hardly expect it to present an unbiased picture of what had taken place. Nevertheless, many of the earliest martyr texts have a down-to-earth air which lends support to their credibility in comparison with the elaborate later hagiographies.

According to the North African writer Tertullian, the governor Saturninus was the first to persecute Christians in Africa. The martyr acts associated with him are not highly evolved literary tracts, but seem like court records, or things noted down by an eyewitness.

17 July 180, council chamber, Carthage. Speratus is the Christians' leader. Saturninus, the governor, tells the accused that they will be reprieved if they swear correctly.

> Speratus: We have never done harm to anyone . . . and we give thanks when ill treated since we hold our emperor in honour.
> Saturninus: We are also a religious people, and our religion is simple, and we swear by the genius of our lord the emperor, and pray for his safety, as you also ought to do.
> Speratus: If you will give me a quiet hearing, I will tell you the mystery of simplicity.

Saturninus: If you begin to speak evil of our sacred rites, I won't give you audience. I ask you to swear by the genius of our lord the emperor.

Speratus: I don't acknowledge this worldly empire, since I serve God who cannot be seen and has never been seen. I have not stolen anything, and if I buy things then I pay the tax because I recognise my Lord, the king of kings and emperor of all peoples.

Saturninus (to the rest): Cease believing in this!

Speratus: Beliefs which say we should murder or lie are evil!

Saturninus (to the rest): Have nothing to do with this madness!

Cittinus: We fear no one but the Lord our God who is in heaven.

The proconsul gave them 30 days to think things over. But they all insisted that they were Christians. So Saturninus read the condemnation. 'They all said, "thanks be to God!" And so they were all crowned with martyrdom together and reign with the Father and the Son and Holy Spirit for ever and ever, Amen."'

From the Roman governor's point of view these people were being astonishingly stubborn, and treasonous, in that they were refusing his and the emperor's authority. In order to maintain his authority, and perhaps in order to pacify the hostile citizenry, the governor may have felt constrained to order execution. To the martyrs, their opponents were in the grip of the Devil and so should be resisted at all costs at the risk of losing their own souls to the underworld. Bystanders may have been heavily hostile to these strange people, yet it is clear that their extraordinary behaviour in the face of something which would ordinarily be terrifying set them apart as special. Moreover, some people could have felt that the penalty being inflicted was unduly harsh.

The attitudes of the Christians themselves were being circulated orally and in written forms. For example, we have the Letter to Diognetus, which is an important Christian apologetic work probably dating from the second or third century AD. Both the person addressed and the author of the work are unknown, but the attitudes are fascinating and clearly expressed. The Letter argues that Christians are just like their fellow citizens in speech and dress, and yet

> . . . they exist in the flesh, but live not after the flesh. They spend their existence on earth, but their citizenship is in heaven. They obey the established laws and in their own lives they surpass the laws. They love all men and are persecuted by all. They are unknown and they are condemned, they are put to death and they gain new life . . . do you not see them flung to the wild beasts to make them deny their God and yet they are unconquered? Do you not see that the more of them are punished the more their numbers increase? These things do not look like the achievements of man; they are the power of God; they are the proofs of His presence.

Christians were charged with 'atheism' since they did not believe in the pagan gods. But it was not so much that they did not believe in them, but that they would not worship them. The pagan gods, for the Christians, were devils, who deluded people and led them into error and evil. Justin, in his *Apology*, wrote:

> old evil demons, effecting apparitions of both defiled men and corrupted boys, which showed such terrifying sights to men that those who did not use reason in judging the actions that were done, were struck with terror, but being carried away by fear and not knowing that these were evil demons, called them gods.

From the second to third centuries Christianity rose from obscurity to become a major topic for serious discussion amongst the chattering classes: they might have called it the 'Christian Problem'. To begin with pagan opinion was ignorant and, when more knowledgeable, dismissive. It was hard for certain intelligent people to take Christians seriously, or to understand that their followers could be anything other than the superstitious, the stupid and the deluded. Unfortunately, texts against Christianity were systematically banned and destroyed by the governments of the Christian empire of late antiquity. We have to rely on quotations preserved in Christian texts refuting these attacks. It is only by this means that we know of Celsus who, recorded by Origen, argued that Christianity was patently absurd.

> While Jesus was alive he did not help himself, but after death he rose again and showed the marks of his punishment and how his hands had been pierced. But who saw this? A hysterical female, as you say, and perhaps some other one of those who were deluded by the same sorcery, who either dreamt in a certain state of mind . . . or what is more likely, wanted to impress the others by telling this fantastic tale.

Celsus was a strongly anti-Christian philosopher living in the second century who wrote a major tract against the sect called the *True Word*. Origen, an influential convert and intellectual, writing *c.*248 answered this with his *Against Celsus*. Celsus sneered at Christianity as being a bizarre provincial superstition of the gullible lower classes. The fact, however, was, as we heard from Pliny, that people of a wide variety of social ranks were Christian believers. Celsus displayed a widespread prejudice of antiquity that philosophy and higher thought were the preserve of the upper classes, were steeped in traditional learning and were anchored in Greek and Roman ideas. Origen, by contrast, argued that a philosopher could quite logically and ethically think within a Christian framework.

Celsus did not deny wonder-working by Christians and by Christ, but he suggested that these were mere illusions, comparing them to the works of sorcerers who profess to do wonderful miracles, who, for a few obols, make known their sacred lore in the middle of the market place and drive demons out of men and blow away diseases and invoke the souls of heroes, and display expensive banquets and dining tables and cakes and dishes which are non-existent, and who make things move as though they were alive although they are not really so, but only appear as such in the imagination.

Celsus, quoted by Origen, says, should we not call such things 'practices of wicked men possessed by an evil daemon'?

Interestingly, this is the very same charge that Christians made of their pagan persecutors. Demons are like angels, spiritual fauna that mediate between the physical and spiritual realms. It is clear for Celsus why the emperor's authority must be upheld, for otherwise 'earthly things would come into the power of the most lawless and savage barbarians'. The Christians, according to him, say Christ would come down and fight. But, Celsus says, how can we believe in that if he refuses to come down and rescue you from *your* present persecution? The Christian response was to say that they fought spiritually for the empire through prayer, to which the pagan response can easily be imagined.

The elite views of Celsus can be understood as reflections of popular preju-dices, many of which are perfectly comprehensible. Christians were not only disliked, but also feared because it was believed that the very existence of Christians angered the gods, as Tertullian in his *Apology* recorded when he exclaimed, 'if the sky doesn't move or the earth does, if there is famine, if there is plague, the cry is at once, "the Christians to the lion!"' Moreover, Christianity was novel and the Roman world was, in many ways, politically, economically and intellectually very conservative. But the prominent Christian writer Clement of Alexandria, in his *Protrepticus*, jibed at such attitudes when he wrote that, if we did not change, we would still be drinking mother's milk.

Anger and fear

The earlier persecutions were really occasional prosecutions. The vibrancy and wide circulation of the martyr acts obscured the fact that the numbers of the executed were very small. This situation was to change with the accession of the emperor Decius, who was born in *c*.201 in what is now Serbia. He ruled from 249 to 251 in a Roman empire that was dramatically changed from that of the previous century. The political stability that had long brought pros-perity to the empire had disintegrated into a period of rapid turnover of military governments, leading to ongoing civil war, decay in frontier security and economic decline. Politics became, if anything, even more ruthless than before and the shedding of blood even more of a routine fact of life.

Decius came to power after killing his predecessor Philip in battle near Verona. The new emperor then marched to the Danube to deal with a substantial invasion of barbarian Goths. This campaign was to occupy him for the rest of his reign and, indeed, was the cause of its ending, for Decius was killed fighting the invaders. He seems to have been convinced that the 'plague' of Christians and the resulting displeasure of the gods was one of the vital factors in the weakening of imperial power. Therefore, at the start of the year 250 he issued an edict ordering all citizens to perform pagan religious sacrifice in the presence of imperial commissioners. In the ensuing trials, large numbers of Christians lapsed, but others, including the bishops of Rome, Jerusalem and Antioch, lost their lives.

From Egypt there are preserved examples of the original documents drawn up by the commissioners as they took oaths.

> [First handwriting] To the commission chosen to superintend the sacrifices at the village of Alexander's Isle. From Aurelius Diogenes, son of Satabous, of the village of Alexander's Isle, aged 72 years, with a scar on the right eyebrow. I have always sacrificed to the gods, and now in your presence in accordance with the edict I have made sacrifice, and poured a libation, and partaken of the sacred victims. I request you to certify this below. Farewell. I, Aurelius Diogenes, have presented this petition.
> [Second handwriting] I, Aurelius Syrus, saw you and your son sacrificing.
> [Third handwriting] illegible (signature of Aurelius?).
> [First Handwriting] This year one of the Emperor Caesar Gaius Messius Quintus Trajanus Decius Pius Felix Augustus, 26 June 250.

The unprecedented thoroughness of this persecution attempt caused shock waves across the empire, not least because it was a vivid expression of imperial power over local communities which, even if pagan, were accustomed to a high degree of local autonomy. However, the swift demise of Decius meant that the prosecutions were not thoroughly completed and his death could be understood as proof of the anger of the Christian God. The presence of large numbers of lapsed Christians may simply have led to widespread guilt at the fact of their weakness in the face of danger and to a strong desire to re-enter the Church and gain absolution. The debate in Africa between those in favour of re-admission and those against became so acrimonious that two separate Churches formed, each of which accused the other of heresy. Decius' attack failed to destroy the Church. After a brief respite, the persecution was continued in the later years of the emperor Valerian (253-60), but discontinued under Gallienus (260-8). There was insufficient persecution to destroy the Christians, but enough to raise their profile dramatically and to suggest the heroism, self-control and self-discipline of their leaders.

Decius was undermined by the weak position of the imperial monarchy during the middle of the third century. From 275 onwards, however, central government began to recover as barbarians were pushed back, and localised foci of regional autonomy were neutralised. A key figure in this process of reconstruction was Diocletian who, ruling at the head of a junta known as the Tetrarchy (rule by four people) from 284–305, was a statesman of genius. Like Decius, Diocletian was a military strongman who wished to use whatever it took to unite the empire under his control. But unlike at the time of Decius, Christianity was not an early target of policy making: what is known as the Great Persecution did not start until the last three years of Diocletian's reign, but it was zealously pursued by his second in command and successor Galerius (305–11). This strongly supports the later Christian writer Lactantius' claim that it was Galerius who was the driving force behind the attempt to wipe out the Christians. This attempt was longer sustained, but no more conclusive than its predecessors.

A flavour of the age comes from the language of late third-century imperial decrees which show a level of superiority and bullying that, perhaps, can only be understood as a reflection of the insecurities of the new political settlement. Non-conformity was denounced and attacked wherever it was identified. For instance, the eastern belief system known as Manichaeism came under attack from Diocletian in an edict of 297. Diocletian said in his decree that the followers of Mani would 'attempt through the accursed morals and savage laws of the Persians to infect men of less wicked nature, i.e. the modest and powerful race of the Romans'. He was at war with Persia and feared Persian contamination. The leaders of the sect were to be burnt and followers to suffer confiscation of their property and committal to the mines. The central point of the decree was that high rank was no longer to be regarded as a protector of persons. Guilt was no longer to be excused by social position. The message was clear. The State was at war with those who were seen as its spiritual, as well as its physical, enemies. The important Christian writer Eusebius was equally savage concerning Mani: 'his very speech and manners proclaimed him a barbarian in mode of life, and being by nature devilish and insane, he suited his endeavours thereto'. Humility and moderation were rapidly vanishing in both pagan and Christian discourse, to be replaced by a heightened language of passion and aggression.

Christianity was also being taken increasingly seriously by pagan intellectuals. By the third century various thinkers were attempting to weld the diverse cults of the pagan world together into a world-explaining system. This so-called Neo-Platonism was a late antique philosophical and emotional celebration of the idea of all goodness as 'emanations' from the 'one God' who is so superior as to be essentially unknowable. Although some were sceptical of such notions, the Roman world in general was possessed of a strong religiosity. Pagan 'high ideas' in late antiquity were vivid meditations on the nature of divinity far removed from the scepticism of earlier imperial writers.

Neo-Platonism considered the physical things of this world and sought to define a path to a superior world that could be perceived, if only with the 'eyes of the mind'. The proximity of such ideas to those held by Christians should be obvious. But whereas Christianity regarded the pagan cults as the work of demons, to pagan philosophers they were so many reflections of the presence of divinity in the world.

People increasingly attempted to make bridges between pagan and Christian ideas. This prompted a counter reaction in the form of sophisticated attempts to deny the validity of any such fusion. Perhaps the greatest attempt to maintain the separation of these intellectual worlds was made by Porphyry, who was born in Tyre in Lebanon, *c.*234, studied in Athens and died in Rome, *c.*305. He completed his most important work, the *Enneads*, in 301; it was a commentary on and edition of the works of the philosopher Plotinus. Surviving fragments in other works of Porphyry's *Against the Christians*, which was condemned to be publicly burnt in 448, show his fierce and incisive criticisms. These are partly philosophical, partly based on logic and partly on attitudes and assumptions prevalent in the ancient world. For instance, Porphyry asked: if Jesus was wise why did he not use eloquence to teach at his trial rather than remaining silent? He also returned to the physically indecorous nature of Christianity:

> Even supposing some Greeks are so foolish as to think that the gods dwell in the statues, even that would be a much purer concept that to admit that the divine providence should descend into the womb of the Virgin Mary, that it became an embryo, and after birth was wrapped in rags, soiled with blood and bile and even worse.

Christ on the cross, for Porphyry, was still little more than a disgusting and humiliated chunk of meat.

Emperors and the Gods

The rise of organised imperial persecution was part and parcel of a change in the nature of rule in the Roman world. The early emperors had been content, in the main, to rule by proxy. Their representatives, the governors, maintained order in the heartland provinces by prosecuting criminals, whilst the army was concentrated in the frontiers to keep out the barbarians. The political instability of the third century made it clear that the loyalty of no area in the empire could be taken for granted. The response of the emperors was to increase the size of the army and institute garrisoning in depth. This was backed up by campaigns of ideological uniformity, of which Christian persecution was a central element. Moreover, the use of splendour in ceremony and dress was steadily enhanced so as to project an image of imperial impregnability and utter superiority.

The history of the rise of such ostentation, which is sometimes referred to as the public 'jewelled' style of the later empire, has to be pieced together from the tantalisingly fragmentary and difficult evidence afforded by the third century. One glimpse is provided by the salary grants in the *Lives of the Emperors* (also known as the *Augustan History*), one of which, to a third-century prince, included two silver-gilt shoulder clasps and one gold, together with a belt, other jewellery, luxury garments, allowances of food, equipment and a retinue of servants. These were given to the future emperor Claudius Gothicus, who was then a legionary commander. The development of imperial splendour was gradual but undeniable and it was accompanied by a heightening of the emperor cult. Imperial imagery was, by the early fourth century, unmistakably evoking the world of divine revelation.

In a Diocletianic fortress at the ancient Egyptian temple at Luxor in Egypt, there has been found a temple of the imperial cult, dating from the first years of the fourth century, from which fragments of plaster paintings survive. Processions of soldiers were shown along the side walls. Opposite the entrance were placed the Tetrarchs amongst their dignitaries, all shown in full frontal perspective. In the apse (niche on the end wall) there was painted an eagle holding a wreath. The Tetrarchs were depicted with a nimbus of light about their heads, and were shown well over life-size and larger than the other figures. Each figure was dressed in precious robes. Similarly, the arch of Galerius at Thessaloniki in northern Greece showed Diocletian and his colleague Maximian during their own lifetimes, enthroned above personifications of earth and sky, in the place of divinity. By this time the emperor was all he could be during his life; death could add nothing. This was the apogee of the imperial cult, in terms of self-expression, even if not in terms of widespread belief – the very fact that there was such a dramatic overstatement of imperial quasi-divinity might suggest a significant level of wider disinterest and disaffection.

But imperial religious policy was not restricted to self-presentation and attacks on subversive cults. Prosperity, happiness and health were no more certain for rulers than they were for anyone else. Emperors fussed incessantly over auspices and auguries. Relations with the true wide immensity of the divine realm were of enormous importance, even to men presented by their propaganda as all-powerful. Bearing in mind the equation of divinity and power and thereby the quasi-divine nature of rule, emperors needed to have consideration for the supernatural. In fact, they had long meddled with it. Throughout the third century various emperors were playing, with steadily greater intensity, on their associations with supreme divinity beyond the bounds of the imperial cult, as when Elegabulus, the high priest of an extraordinary eastern cult, became emperor. During the latter half of the third century, the majesty of sublime *Sol* the sun god played over the imperial palace. The Tetrarchs were explicitly associated with Jove and Hercules. It had become quite normal for emperors to have a novel religious 'policy' and in this sense Constantine, who was to embrace Christianity, can be seen to have acted in accordance with the traditions of his time.

Why did Christianity grow?

This is one of the classic questions of European history and one to which there cannot be a simple or final answer. A recent approach to the subject is interesting for the fact that it comes from a statistically minded sociologist, rather than, more conventionally, from the textual analysis of an ecclesiastical historian. Rodney Stark published his ideas in *The Rise of Christianity: A Sociologist Reconsiders History* (Princeton, 1996), which has since generated much critical discussion.

There is a key problem of perceived inevitability: the idea that because Europe converted, it was fated to convert. One can suggest that there are major accidents in history which push events to their conclusion. The conversion of Constantine is one of those, although Stark provides images of steady expansion, suggesting that something fundamental and structural was taking place and so implying that Christianity was a product that increasing numbers of people would wanted to buy in any case. Stark uses a comparative example, contemporary Mormon expansion, which has run at 40 per cent per decade to suggest figures for the ancient world.

Year	Number of Christians	% of the Empire's population
40	1000	0.0017
50	1400	0.0023
100	7,500	0.0126
150	40,000	0.07
200	218,000	0.36
250	1,171,000	1.9
300	6,300,000	10.5
350	33,900,000	56.5

(after Stark, p.7)

Our author gives a strong defence of such comparative models, saying that they are essential to science since the particular in its singularity is meaningless: 'consider a physics that must generate a new rule of gravity for every object in the universe' (p.23). And it is, of course, impossible to work entirely without comparative models, since everything must be judged from some comparative viewpoint and historical study cannot avoid being judgmental if only in considering what and what not to study.

Stark argues that the rise of early Christianity, like modern Mormonism, was rooted in personal interrelationships and the support that the Church gave to people in their social lives. The failure of the Roman State's opposition, he argues, was based on lack of willpower. It did not persecute thoroughly. It tended to pick off leaders and leave hangers-on untouched. Christianity was treated as something where leaders could be killed and their executions would provide proof of failure. But, of course, Christianity was distinctively perverse in that what was traditionally seen as proof of failure was viewed as proof of success. The steadfastness of the Christians in that belief was, ultimately, stronger than others' disbelief. The reason for that is fairly straightforward: Christians who were not steadfast in their belief in the resurrection of Jesus were simply not Christians. And pagans were, by nature, less fixed in their beliefs, since their spiritual world was a place full of unpredictable and, possibly, unknowable forces. Therefore, there was always a sense in which pagans tended to think that it was important to give unusual religious views the benefit of the doubt.

Christianity, argues Stark, was not the religion of the downtrodden. It was, in many ways, an urban and elite cult. It was esoteric, and may have appealed particularly to those with a good deal of money who could thus give wealth away in a dramatic manner. The Christian mission to the Jews may not have been a failure. The locations of the cities where Christianity first arose show clear parallels with the distribution of the Jewish communities of the Diaspora. Judaism, therefore, can be seen as providing a seedbed for expansion of Christianity into the pagan communities.

Christians, Stark contends, may have been able to raise larger families due to nursing being an important element of Christian charity and because of the duty to feed the sick. A further issue is the killing of unwanted female children in pagan families, which was discouraged by the Church. This led to a comparative abundance of females with Christian parents, who might then grow up to be attracted to the Church because it could give them greater status than they found in traditional society. They married pagan men, and brought the children up as Christian. The rise of virginity in the Church may, however, have been some check on this process.

Stark also provides a strong image of ancient cities as alarming places in which there was a chaos of different beliefs and a lack of social provision. 'I began to realise that all the cities of the empire were incredibly disorganised, even compared with the rapidly growing and industrializing cities of the nineteenth century, the ones that caused early sociologists to express endless doom and gloom' (p.144). Stark's towns are overwhelmingly full of heaving, sordid tenements, rather than the grand houses of the Hollywood imagination. The sewers did not reach most places, and the cisterns on which supply relied would have been breeding grounds for disease. This is very different from the visions of vibrancy and opulence which are frequently projected in relation to ancient urban centres. He locates Christianity as an urban salvation movement and, certainly, official Christianisation, when it arrived in the fourth century, was projected out from the towns to the countryside (which was, in many areas, still then the place of stubborn paganism).

Martyrdom is seen by Stark as a rational choice: it was simply that people made different estimations of value. Personal glory and immortality were a heady mixture. Moreover, the key fact is that there were not many martyrs, and people who did not push things to the final sacrifice were not remembered or remarked upon. The role of self-denial in ancient Christianity meant that this was a heroic level of commitment which was above that possible for ordinary Christians. And yet they, through charity, were nevertheless enabled to do their bit without feeling ashamed. Martyrdom occurred in public, before a large audience, and was 'often the culmination of a long period of preparation during which those faced with martyrdom were the object of intense, face-to-face adulation' (p.180).

Stark's figures can be easily contested. They are derived from a very different age and context; nevertheless, they do seem to mirror the stages of the emergence of Christianity from obscure sect, to significant problem, to majority religion. However, Stark is right insofar as we need to think in terms of the benefits brought by Christianity — it must have provided things which were not available via traditional pagan cults. It provided a community organisation in which people of all stations and both genders could find an appropriate position. It provided a unified explanation for the world and its history, the understanding of which did not require an elaborate philosophical education. It provided the opportunity for hero worship of the martyrs, and of healing through miracles provided by their relics. And above all, Christianity provided the promise of an afterlife of bliss in heaven, whereas the pagans thought that only the greatest souls would soar up to dwell as stars in the skies. Moreover, Christianity was exclusive. Conversion was intended as a one-way trip. You could not be fickle in your devotions as was the case with the pagan cults.

Sections of Stark's analysis are based on sweeping assumptions: for example, 'to anyone raised in a Judeo-Christian or Islamic culture, the pagan gods seem almost trivial. Each is but one of a host of gods and godlings of very limited scope, power and concern' (p.211). The rise of the empire, and the movement of people across Europe to fight in its armies, forced local communities to reinterpret the extraordinary variety of local religious expressions. As the cities' independence faded, so perhaps did their personal gods and goddesses. An empire-wide religious solution was possibly needed by ordinary people to make sense of this new wider world. However, the limited power of the pagan deities may have found a mirror in the cult of the saints which acted to bridge the emerging gap between the local and the general, suggesting that this was a world which required both forms of religious expression.

Philosophy seems to have been moving in this very direction, perhaps influenced by Christianity, or under the pressure of the same psychological and political realities. Pagan thought was, however, self-consciously intellectual and exclusive. It was all about elite ideas and study. It was a world separated from the realm of mass culture. The power of the mystery cults, especially Christianity, was that they provided the scope for spectacular community worship, for personal devotions and also for philosophical and intellectual speculation and analysis should that be your particular bent. The propaganda of Christianity was remorseless. Only Christ could offer eternal life. The deep fear of death and the incomprehension of much traditional classical thought concerning what lay beyond the grave were important factors in the success of the Church, especially when combined with the Christian assertion that abandoning the faith or combining it with others would lead to eternal suffering.

Beyond that, a crucial factor was that Christianity *did* compromise with the mores and values of contemporary society. The notion of the just war legit-imised killing and rich people were accepted into the Church without having to give away all their wealth. Despite, or partly because of, the persecutions, Christianity had achieved a dynamic momentum of growth by the end of the third century. The ignorance and dismissal of earlier times was simply no longer an option, whilst fear and anger had resulted in an uneasy stalemate.

4 The Empire takes control

Invested as he is with the semblance of heavenly sovereignty, he directs his gaze above, and frames his earthly government according to the pattern of the divine original, feeling strength in its conformity to the monarchy of God.

Eusebius, *Oration on the Tricennalia of Constantine*, AD 336

Constantine, like Pilate, is known through the words and opinions of others. And, like Pilate, it is hard to tell vision from reality. What is quite clear is that Constantine's actions were to be more important for the future development of Europe than those of almost any other emperor. He moved the capital of the empire to the Greek east, to Byzantium (the city of Constantine, Constantinopolis, Constantinople, modern Istanbul). The eastern Roman Empire was to remain whilst the west collapsed, resulting in that 1000-year kingdom known to modern historians, if not to its inhabitants who called themselves Romoioi (Romans), as the Byzantine Empire. Constantine also embraced Christianity.

Here we can easily get into fruitless speculation: what would have happened if Constantine had not won out in the complex series of wars he was forced to fight? Would there have been persecuting pagan emperors instead? Would that have resulted in Christianity's extinction? We, obviously, cannot know, and yet this begs a further fascinating question: was the victory of Christianity based on its inherent appeal to the masses, or was imperial conversion necessary to sell it to the upper classes?

Constantine was, as we have seen, radical. And yet he was not completely original. Nero had dreamt feverishly of rebuilding Rome atop a mountain. Other emperors pursued unorthodox religious and personal behaviour. Amongst the lurid rumours in the *Augustan History* concerning the third-century emperor Eliogabulus was that he 'asserted that all the gods were merely servants of his [Syrian] god, calling some its chamberlains, some its slaves, and yet others its attendants for various things'. Constantine needs to be understood in the context of a system of imperial rule that gave to successful incumbents an extraordinary degree of power and authority that would be any megalomaniac's dream. Above all, his actions need to be set against the unusual circumstances of the Tetrarchy, the junta system that Constantine effectively dismantled.

Perhaps as extraordinary as Constantine's actions was an event on 1 May 305. Diocletian, the soldier-emperor and creator of the Tetrarchic system,

7   *Fragments of a colossal statue of Constantine, front view and detail*

retired to a fortified palace at Split. His co-emperor, Maximian, did the same thing, retiring to Lucania in southern Italy. Diocletian had seen the centrifugal forces that were pulling the vast empire apart and one of his solutions was to create a regional system of emperors, who would be tied together via intermarriage. So confident was Diocletian in the stability of this new system that he felt able to step down from public life.

However, emperors did not just resign. Once out of power they lost control of the armies and were an obvious target for assassination. Diocletian did choose to retire to a fortress (albeit a very nicely decorated seaside one), but he must have retained some measure of military control. There was, however, political confusion, and Diocletian briefly came out of retirement when he was offered the chance of a return to power, only to decline it on 11 November 308, saying that he preferred to live quietly and grow cabbages. We do not know when he died, but no one claims he was killed.

The problem with the Tetrarchy was that it only worked if there was trust and balance of power between the members. This did not persist without the dominating presence of Diocletian. A protracted civil war was fought amongst various leaders, some of whom clung to his policies of division of rule and persecution of Christians, and some, notably Constantine, who did not.

It is clear that, by this date, a policy toward Christianity, that rapidly spreading group which would not swear allegiance to the divinity of the emperors, was of prime importance. As we have seen, Christianity was no longer restricted to particular regions and was certainly not limited to an underclass. Decades earlier emperor Alexander Severus had kept statues of Abraham, Orpheus, Christ and Apollonius of Tyana in his private chapel, to which, according to Eusebius, he paid equal respect. Porphyry, whilst making massive criticisms of Christianity, found Christ outstanding as a man, stating that 'we should not speak ill of Christ but should pity the folly of mankind'.

This was an age framed by the Decian persecution of 249-50 and by the Tetrarchic persecutions which Constantine halted. Christianity was spreading widely through the third century causing the Roman government to sit up and take notice. It was clear during these years that Christianity could no longer be ignored. It had the expansionary force which the diverse collection of sects called paganism seemed to lack. The response involved a transformation of pagan thought as in the development of monotheistic Neo-Platonist ideas. Pagan prophets and martyrs were sought. Apollonius of Tyana, for example, was touted as a rival to Christ by men like Hierocles, a provincial governor active in the Tetrarchic Persecution. Such thinking gave paganism its own cadre of professional priests and miracle-workers. This is not to suggest that paganism was moribund, but that Christianity seemed to be generating the excitement to which pagan thinkers were being forced to respond.

Ultimately, the creation of the empire may have had a key role to play in this process. While Europe was a constellation of different cities, each was unproblematically under the protection of its patron deity. The problem came when people started to move round, as when they were in the army. When there were patently so many deities available it was hard to know which way to turn, or whom to believe. A distinction seems to have opened up between the concept of a creative force, the great deity in the sky, and lesser spirits who helped individuals with their daily concerns. Many people in Christian late antiquity could continue to believe that the One ruled over life and death on a grand scale and, as such, was the concern of emperors, but that everyday matters were still in the hands of lesser gods, saints, demons and angels.

Both Constantine and his father seem to have believed in a form of solar monotheism. Apollo was the pagan sun god. There was a long history to this form of worship. Caligula and Nero were both proclaimed Neos Helios. A colossal statue of Sol Apollo was erected outside Nero's Golden House with a radiant crown. Aurelian, in the third century, had been a devotee of Sol Invictus (the Unconquered Sun). In an anonymous panegyric on Constantine in 310 the emperor, prior to battles in Gaul, is described as seeing a temple vision of Apollo and Victory offering laurel crowns, the former being described as Constantine's 'patron god'. It is not known quite where this temple was. It may have been at Grand on the border between the provinces of Belgica and Germania Superior. The temple of Apollo Grannus there was a healing cult associated with springs where cures often occurred after a vision.

Galerius, the Tetrarch who had been driving persecution of Christians, issued a toleration edict in 311, stating that 'it will be their duty to pray to their god for our good estate, and that of the State, and their own, that the commonwealth may endure on every side unharmed, and they may be able to live securely'. Lactantius, writing a century later, says that Galerius had fallen ill by the will of God and that is what prompted his rethink. Meanwhile, his colleague Maximin went along with, but seemingly did not approve of, this alteration of policy. He was busy trying to develop and revive pagan worship on a quasi-Christian model. Provincial high priests were established, each with a guard of soldiers, and beneath them there were to be subordinate priests in each city. This was clearly an attempt to systematise pagan worship and tie it closely to the State, to end the earlier situation where paganism had been essentially very localised.

It is also Lactantius who tells us that Constantine had a dream in 312 in which he was told to place a sign of Christ on the shields of his soldiers and that he would then win. The story, told 25 years after the event by Eusebius (who heard it on oath from Constantine), was that a cross appeared in the sky with 'by this sign you will conquer' written round it. The next night there came a vision of a figure saying 'place the heavenly sign on the battle standards'. Constantine was successful in driving his opposer, Maxentius, from Italy and in 313 he issued the Edict of Milan. This was ostensibly done in order to foster the peace of the times, establish complete toleration for all beliefs, and allow for restitution of property seized in the persecutions. At the same time Constantine made grants of cash to clergy and confirmed their

8 & 9   *Colossal image of a late Roman emperor which may have originally been erected on*
a pillar in Constantinople, now in Barletta, Italy

8   *(left) The soldier emperor would originally have held a spear or the* labarum
(imperial banner) in his right hand

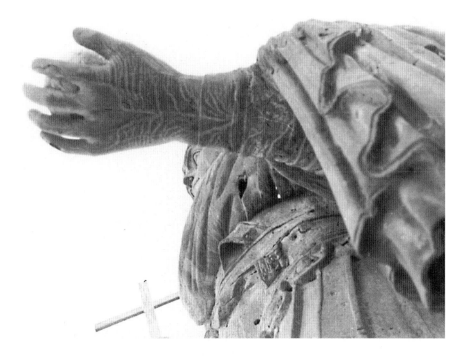

9   Detail of image. The left fist holds the world in the form of a globe

10　*Christ depicted as a soldier emperor, mosaic, Archiepsicopal chapel, Ravenna, as the
Church adopted imperial imagery (late fifth century)*

11 *Mosaic of the archangel Michael also dressed as an emperor, Sant' Apollinare in Classe, Ravenna (early sixth century)*

*12   Constantine looks to the heavens on this gold medallion of AD 306-37, minted in
Siscia, Croatia.* Copyright British Museum

exemption from public office: 'for when they render supreme service to the
deity, it seems that they confer incalculable benefit on the affairs of the State'.

This was not an unambiguously Christian edict. Above all, there is nothing
in it that attacks paganism (which was the cult of devils, according to the
Church). There was only a gradual appearance of explicitly Christian imagery
on Constantine's coins. The 315 Arch of Constantine in Rome is studiously
neutral in its language and imagery. He continued to hold the office of
Pontifex Maximus (pagan chief priest of Rome). He was also not baptised
until shortly before his death, although this is not that unusual in the ancient
world. Constantine's new capital at Byzantium was not thoroughly
Christianised. New temples were built to Victory and the Greek mother
goddess Rhea. The new churches of the city, Sacred Wisdom, Sacred Peace
and Sacred Power (Hagia Sophia, Hagia Eirene and Hagia Dynamis) were, in
their dedications, highly comprehensible to pagans. The cult of the martyrs
was conspicuous only by its marginalisation. Moreover, Constantine had a
massive image of himself erected in the city, glittering in gold and purple and
adorned with the attributes of solar worship, whilst below devotees sang

hymns to the sun god. Constantine's coinage was wont to show him staring upwards to heaven, a pose emphasised by Eusebius in the opening quotation to this chapter. Yet that image was a copy of one used for Alexander the Great who, along with Augustus, was the archetype of classical monarchy.

One way in which to understand Constantine is to say that either he was unsure of his religious beliefs, or he was unsure of the support of the empire. He can be understood as possessing a mixture of ideas in which Christianity was mingled with pagan solar worship, since the Christian God was located as lording over the heavens. Only, as his reign progressed, and he received the teachings of his biographer and bishop Euesbius and other confidants, may his understanding have clarified. But more than this, the plain fact is that the majority of his empire was pagan. However successful and megalomaniac Constantine may have been, politics required a degree of compromise. This may, of course, have changed rapidly, as the number of converts soared during the course of the fourth century.

Golden gifts

The persecutions had backfired on the persecutors, since Christians won a reputation as heroes and spiritual champions. In modern jargon the whole process turned into a major PR disaster for the government. In fact the bad publicity seems to have been out of all proportion to the numbers killed, especially bearing in mind that persecution was highly sporadic, only reaching peaks in the mid-third century and the early fourth. As Peter Brown has pointed out, 'what is certain is that there is no room for the later Romantic myth of Christians as a perpetually hounded minority, literally driven underground by unremitting persecution.'

Nor was it a poor religion solely of the underprivileged. It is to the formal end of persecution and the architectural legacy of Constantine that we can attribute the major boost to monumentality in Christian worship. Aristocrats were then encouraged by imperial example to convert and act as patrons of the Church. Yet the church at Dura Europos shows us the richness of some third-century Christian decoration. And whilst there is no doubt that Constantine played an enormously important role in financially endowing the Church, there are clear signs that the faith had been developing in that direction long before. The issue of the rich Christian had been an important one for the early Church. The consensus view from the third century was that the rich were not to be rejected but that their wealth was to be channelled to good causes through charity. This might, it was believed, rightly take the form of gifts to the poor, or it could be achieved through the endowment and construction of churches that were meeting halls for the community and places where lavish spending could be said to be an offering directly to God.

Early 'house churches' were originally dwellings of Christians which were used for services. Over time, as congregations grew, the buildings came to be adapted and enlarged. Eusebius talked of these as 'meeting places' (*conventicula*), but he also used the generic term for churches, *ecclesia*, and also, on occasion, described them as being basilicas (public meeting halls). At the very end of the third century or the beginning of the fourth a big basilican hall was erected at Aquilaea. This suggests that, even without the example of Constantine, people were beginning to build imposing public buildings for the faithful. We also know that many churches possessed not only books but also gold and silver liturgical objects. At Cirta in North Africa, in 303, there was a government raid on a small church. The record of the confiscated silver plate survives. Furthermore, Prudentius, in his poem, *Crowns of Martyrdom*, describes the avarice of a local official who was driven to persecution by greed. Demanding that the riches of a particular church be delivered up, he was shown a group of virgins who were described as 'spiritual silver'. This example suggests that churches were thought of by the authorities as stores of wealth. The very presence of wealth in the churches may have been an additional motivation for persecution by central government, as well as on the part of corrupt local officials, since the treasury was always seeking new sources of revenue.

Traditionally, it has been thought – if we deny the image of an impoverished sect – that the paucity of Christian imagery prior to the later third century derives from the inherited Jewish suspicion of images. There are, however, two important qualifications to be made on this point. Firstly, Christians were few in the early decades and so we can hardly expect to find a wide range of buildings and artefacts associated with them. In other words, the small number of early Christians makes them less likely to appear prominently in the archaeological record. Secondly, Judaism, during the period of Roman control, saw synagogues become ever more elaborately decorated, as fashions from the wider Graeco-Roman world permeated the fringes of the empire. Even figural art appeared in certain synagogues. And, beyond that, it should be remembered that many Jews were living at the heart of towns across the empire and may have had to rely on gentile artists and craftsmen. Christian hostility to art and monumentality was, in fact, muted. The Jewish prohibition on graven images was generally rejected. Although there were to be violent disputes between iconoclasts (breakers of images) and iconodules (defenders of images), above all during the early to middle Byzantine period, the Christian churches largely accepted images. They tended to understand them not as objects of worship themselves but as tools with which to lead and teach the mind.

The traditions of Roman art and splendour were laid at the disposal of the Church on the grandest scale by Constantine. The buildings which he ordered to be constructed were frequently based upon traditional Roman audience halls, or meeting halls. This basilican plan was very different to the closed and restricted form of classical temples. These churches were intended to house worshippers meeting within rather than without. And, as such, they afforded tremendous scope for interior decoration and ostentation, since they were conceived as being the audience chambers of God. Constantine was keen to show that he was heavily committed to his project of conversion and so he wished for no expense to be spared.

Where did the money come from? This was an emperor who trod with ever more conviction as he became more secure in power. The problem is that our sources are frequently later in date and are marked by partisan Christian and pagan approaches. The pagans tend to accuse Constantine of vast financial profligacy, of which the building of churches was simply a single element, and of accompanying rapacity. Sozomen tells us of the seizing of temple hoards, during which pagan priests 'offered their most precious treasures, even those icons called Heaven-Sent, and these objects emerged from the sacred recesses and hiding places in the temples . . . and became public property'. We are talking here about precious objects which would have been deposited as votive offerings to the gods. People placed their family names on these gold and silver vessels, and so this can be seen as an attack not just on the cults, but on cities and their local elites. This sort of ruthlessness is fully in keeping with the atmosphere and practices of the Tetrarchy amongst which Constantine had grown up. Whilst he did not close the temples, he did regulate behaviour, decreeing, for example, that the eunuch priests of Egypt and 'every species of androgyne should be exterminated as a sort of monstrosity'. The results of the conversion of Constantine emerged, overall, as exercises in power and imperial will that were far more effective than the previous persecutions had been. Constantine gave Christians huge new opportunities for display, whilst, allegedly, stripping these from the pagans. The exclusive nature of Christian worship acted to trap people once they had converted and so the backdrop was set for the dramatic growth of what was now the State cult.

Cyril Mango has written that, in speaking of 'early Christian art . . . we must remember that we mean the art of the later Roman Empire adapted to the needs of the Church'. The prestige of the emperors was lent to churches which were built and decorated in the grandest imperial style. Pagans were drawn in by the splendour of the luxuriously fitted churches of the great cities. During this period the word *aula*, which along with *palatium* meant 'palace', was commonly applied to churches. Architecturally, palace and church basilicas were very similar in form, as they were in decoration. It is hardly surprising, therefore, to find the similarity extending to the language of the age, which as Krautheimer attests, 'establishes the church as the throne room of the emperor of heaven: comparable to the sanctuary where the living God-emperor received the obeisance of his subjects'. Expensive display was widely understood as being appropriate in the context of divinity so as to show proper respect. It would take great courage to attack this extraordinary alliance of physical, symbolic and spiritual power. The broad consensus was that God and the emperor were masters of the physical world and, therefore,

13   *The splendour of late Roman churches: nave, Santa Maria Maggiore, Rome.*
Copyright Leo Curran, Maecenas Archive

it was right that power be so materially displayed and celebrated with that characteristic public monumentality of which Roman architects were such past masters. After all, such property was public and, thus, individuals were preserved from the sin of personal greed.

This was a slightly uneasy solution, however. Ripples of discontent occasionally rose to the surface, most notably from the acerbic pen of St Jerome. An ascetic, famous for not pulling his punches, he wrote condemning painters, sculptors, stonemasons and other 'minions of dissoluteness'. He commented on Jesus' words, 'consider the lilies of the field, how they grow; they toil not, neither do they spin: yet I say to you that even Solomon in all his glory was not arrayed like one of these', by asking, 'what silk, what royal purple, what weaving patterns can be compared with flowers? . . . The eyes even more than words, pronounce that no other purple matches the purple of the violet.' Many build churches these days, Jerome tells us, that shine with marbles and glitter with gold, their altars studded with gems, while little attention is paid to the choice of Christ's ministers. It is of no concern that the Temple in ancient Judaea was bright with gold, for that was when priests offered up victims and 'the blood of sheep was the redemption of sins'.

A similar line of criticism comes from an early fifth-century tract which seems to be derived from the British heretical sect known as the Pelagians. This piece, known simply as *On Riches*, demands, 'let there be an end to false allegory, now that we are furnished with the truth and now that it is not the approval of the reader that we are seeking but his improvement'. Texts of the Old Testament such as that describing the Temple and the Tabernacle make abundant mention of elaborate decorations in gold and silver. The orthodox position was that these references were allegorical descriptions of spiritual wealth and excellence. By contrast the heretical writer of *On Riches* denounces those who use these texts to defend riches. The documents of suppressed heresies are rarely preserved. This tract, therefore, offers an invaluable and rare glimpse of the opinions of those who felt that the orthodox view was a betrayal of Christ's Word, and that an institution which preached against worldly splendour should not be similarly ostentatious itself through dependence on the charity of rulers and aristocrats.

But it is clear that the multicoloured churches were enormously popular with patrons, priests and worshippers. Partly, this is because ostentation had been an aspect of much pagan worship and so was expected by the converts. Christianity must needs have addressed the whole world and not merely that portion of mankind with which it found communication most easy. Treasures communicated to the mass of society and symbolic understanding provided the tool to enable treasure metaphor to be identified with Christian salvation. This world was one in which the Church revelled in its victory. It was triumphantly, unashamedly rich. It was not simply that massive basilicas were going up in the cities of the empire. Luxury materials were carefully applied to vestments, liturgical equipment and texts. The holy of holies itself, the very words of Holy Scripture, were transcribed in gold and silver ink onto expensive purple parchment and bound in jewelled covers. Examples of this include the sixth-century Codex Petropolitanus from Asia Minor. This has the text written in silver, with the names of God and Jesus in gold (other similar examples from late antiquity include the Vienna Genesis and the Rossano and Synope Gospels).

All of this does *seem* to be very far removed from the message of Jesus. However, the Church establishment did not find a problem with this. It was seeking to fulfil the message of Jesus as then understood. Jesus said, 'do not lay up for yourselves treasures on earth, where moth and rust consume and where thieves break in and steal, but lay up for yourselves treasures in heaven, where neither moth nor rust consumes and where thieves do not break in and steal'. The Church said exactly the same thing *to individuals*, since it understood Jesus to have been talking to individual people. The splendour of the Church itself was a very different matter. That institution was the agent of God on earth. God had legitimised matter through Jesus' human incarnation. However, if Jesus left abundant testimony for rules on personal behaviour, he did not spell out how to run a major organisation of churches other than with the example of the disciples who held all their possessions in common. This was exactly what the late antique church believed it was doing. Christian writers of that age were, by and large, perfectly sincere men and women who lived in a world far closer to that of Jesus than is our own. Who are we to say that their interpretation of Scripture was inferior to ours?

Of course there may also have been an element of wishful thinking. Bishops were probably not keen to deny gifts of money once the imperial regime had finally become favourable. Furthermore, there is the basic issue of practicality. It is not clear that Constantine would accept refusal of his donations. Doubters could reflect on the emperor's success and conclude that what he was doing must be right since he was helped and favoured by God. Moreover, there was a strongly combined aesthetic and spiritual impetus towards magnificence. Churches were intended as the closest possible recreation of heaven, both in the sanctity of those gathered there and in the very experience of being in the place. Art in these buildings was intended to impress and instruct the viewer and to do honour directly to God and indirectly to the donors. An appealing vision of the Christian paradise was of enormous importance in the spread of the religion, because the promise of that place was the greatest thing that Christianity could offer. Classical metaphors of excellence focused upon great quantity and high quality. Images of luxuriant nature could portray abundance. Light could represent the concept of sublime purity. Gold could represent both ideals. All these elements were made use of in the physical construction of the Christian view of paradise. Scriptural employment legitimated all these modes of the presentation of excellence through abundant references to past splendour in Israel. Precedents for the use of nature, light and precious metals could easily be found in the repertoire of classical visual art.

Public life in the later Roman empire was characterised by an intensified use of jewellery and magnificence. There is no break in this regard between the periods before and after the imperial conversion to Christianity. Grand display was an act of communication which advanced the status of the participants. Such was the importance of these displays and the significance of the messages that they conveyed that the State regulated the use of gold and gems by officials. The government and army were represented by a carefully constructed system of uniforms and insignia that displayed the status hierarchy of the sacred State (*sacra res publica*). Such official costumes made ever more intense use of silk, expensive purple dyes and gold decoration. The emperor himself might be shown in military costume, but always with such grand adornments as a jewelled helmet. Or he might be shown dressed in a toga, but one made of purple-dyed silk sewn with gold and gems (the imperial *trabea*). His cloak (*chlamys*) would be more splendid than anyone else's and it was held at the shoulder by a huge brooch of a design worn by no one outside the imperial household. He was also shown with a jewelled diadem. This was a totalitarian regime and, as with much of the official art of the major twentieth-century dictatorships, the leader's individuality came to be subsumed into an all-encom-passing image of power. As Golomstock wrote in connection with Hitler and Stalin, the leader became a 'figure of allegory'. And as Ramsay MacMullen has commented, late antiquity was an age in which 'importance thus expressed itself in a man's outward appearance . . . An emperor should look like an emperor and should be identifiable by his shoes or by the hem of his mantle'.

Dressed in this fashion, it is hardly surprising the emperors chose to reside in buildings of an equivalent magnificence. This display was clung to at the heart of the Byzantine empire even during its very lean period after the Arab expansion of the seventh century. The wonderful show of those palaces comes to us at several removes in Yeats' *Sailing to Byzantium*, but more contemporaneously from the testimony of Corippus in the sixth century and from the later *De Ceremoniis* (*On Ceremonies*), the fond and somewhat Gormenghastly testimony of emperor Constantine Porphyrogenitus. Such ostentation might seem seriously out of keeping if we go by the testimony of the writers of the earlier Empire. Nero and other 'bad emperors' were castigated by Suetonius and Tacitus for such display which they found excep-tional, eastern-influenced and 'un-Roman'. Yet this may be somewhat biased. Parallels from the earliest years of imperial greatness can be found. The word 'palace' (*palatium*) itself derives from the Palatine Hill where Augustus lived. The transference of meaning from Palatine to Palace is already visible in the poetry of the early Principate. Augustus always claimed an image of modesty, yet such rhetoric probably acted to play down what was likely to have been a rather grand sort of home.

What was really being done to decorate the homes of the Augustan elite is hard to establish because of the fragmentary nature of the archaeological evidence. Gold and jewels are not normally left around a house for several centuries in expectation of the arrival of modern and scientific archaeolo-gists. Nevertheless, there are some fascinating survivals. One such example was exhibited in 1986 in Rome. This consisted of a display of 400 jewels that once adorned the walls or ceiling of a room in a first-century town house that came into the possession of Caligula. Romans of this time, whilst publicly claiming frugality, may have imitated the splendours of the Hellenistic Greek monarchs whose power had been displaced by the expanding empire. It is clear that not only emperors, but also senators, were inspired by and, perhaps, were exceeding these models. For example, the mad buildings, the '*insania*', of Scaurus under the late Republic were referred to later as having 'outdone the worst excesses of Nero and Caligula'. Such flamboyance was, by these actions, slowly being 'made Roman' long before it was to escalate into the full-blown elite style of the late empire.

The fall of Nero's government lead to the destruction of his Golden House in which 'everything was overlaid with gold and adorned with gems and mother-of-pearl'. Nevertheless, this was only a temporary setback. Later Roman and Byzantine palaces have been the subject of considerable investi-

14   Audience hall of the imperial palace, early fourth century, Trier

gation, much of which has focused either upon examination of ground plans, or upon study of literary evidence. Other work has investigated the development of specific elements of palaces such as the Vestibule of the Great Palace at Constantinople, basilican throne-rooms and *triclinia* (grand dining rooms). In the city of Byzantium there were several palaces some of which were in the centre of town and others outside it. But there, as at Rome, archaeological survival has not been of an encouraging level because these ruins were obvious targets for pillaging. One of the best-preserved imperial palace audience halls is that at Trier. Dating from the early fourth century, this huge building, 67m long by 30m high, was originally part of a massive complex of buildings. Archaeological investigation has found traces of the original gold mosaic decoration. When the Church became incorporated into the State, churches in just this basilican form were built both in palace complexes and at places where martyrs' bodies were buried (such as St Peter's in Rome).

As a part of his promotion of Christianity as the State religion in the early fourth century, the emperor Constantine did honour to his God by showering the Church with gifts in the form of estates, cash, buildings and

*15 & 16   The cross, by the sixth century, had been transformed from a symbol of disgrace into
           a jewelled emblem of triumph*

15   Vault mosaic, Archiepiscopal Chapel, Ravenna

vast numbers of gold and silver treasures. Gifts to San Giovanni in Laterano, for example, included over 50 gold vessels weighing over 400lb, with gold foil for the apse weighing 500lb. Having originated in poverty, Christianity had taken up a dominant place in the social world of the Roman Empire. In that process, use of goods and substances particular to the social elite came to be employed by the Church in pursuit of its own self-promotion. Not all Christians approved of this process, as we have seen with Jerome: 'I do not find fault with those who made the change for the sake of honour, nor with those that made the gold vessels for the Temple, but I wonder that the Lord, Creator of the Universe, was born not surrounded by gold and silver, but by mud.' But he was an exception. Most Christians appear to have revelled in the new and huge wealth of the Church. The acceptance of the jewelled splendour of these churches was bolstered by the Jewish heritage of treasure decoration, as preserved in the sacred words of the Old Testament. In late antique texts, the golden ornaments both of the ancient Jewish Temples and of the new churches were described in terms of their wonderful glitter and brilliance, symbolic of the splendour of God and the brightness of Christian love.

16 *Apse mosaic, Sant'Apollinare in Classe, Ravenna*

The extensive corpus of gold mosaics from the period, especially from Italy, provides one of the best sources of evidence for Christian use of this metal in art. At some point during the imperial period metallic *tesserae* (mosaic tiles) were invented. These came to be employed under the late empire in ever-larger numbers. Their popularity appears to have been inspired by the same impetus that led to the extensive use of gilding on wood, stucco and marble. Metallic *tesserae* were manufactured by placing a thin film of silver or gold upon a sheet of glass, over which a second layer of glass was poured. By the fourth and fifth centuries gold *tesserae* were being employed on a considerable scale as a colour in place of yellow. An example of this occurs in the scene of Joshua fighting the five Amorite Kings in Santa Maria Maggiore. However, during late antiquity, a new phenomenon appeared that was to remain a prominent aspect of a very large proportion of medieval western and eastern mosaic art. This was the use of gilt *tesserae* to provide the illusion of a solid gold background. Perhaps the best early surviving example of such large-scale gold grounds are the late fourth-century apse mosaics from Sant'Aquilino, Milan. In the early Middle Ages such gold ground can be found displacing many of the elaborate decorative motifs favoured by Roman taste, a trend that was to lead to the full golden style that can be seen in medieval Italian and Byzantine churches. These works of art would have glittered down above precious metal vessels and revetments which, by contrast, have rarely been preserved in situ.

Precious metal treasures

Finds of gold and silver objects are among the most high-profile discoveries from the later Roman period. Those assemblages that survive have done so because they were hidden in the ground for safe-keeping. Because these substances have retained their high value in modern society we can appreciate the importance they possessed in the empire. Assemblages of such objects, especially of silverware, are popularly referred to as 'treasures'. Although silver plate is a prominent category of late antique treasure, other items are often discovered at the same time, including jewellery and coins as well as scraps of precious metal.

Art historical sources provide us with evidence of these items in contemporary use, for example the women's jewellery shown on the frescoes found under Trier cathedral, and mosaics, such as those of Santa Maria Maggiore in Rome and of San Vitale in Ravenna, which show abundant treasure items. In the latter case, Justinian and Theodora are shown bringing offerings of precious plate to the altar. They and their entourage feature a variety of prominent and distinctive jewellery which parallels finds from the period. Display was a crucial element of the function of these items. Silverware might well be kept on public view in an aristocrat's house even when it was not in

17 Apse mosaics, sixth century, San Vitale, Ravenna

use for a banquet. From the earlier empire, a fresco at Pompeii shows such a set placed on a *repositorium* (viewing table), the status symbol of a wealthy and doubtless fashionable local magistrate.

Objects in precious metal, by virtue of their cost, were prestige objects and their possession the preserve of elite elements in society. This is not to say that poorer people may not have possessed the occasional silver clasp, for example, but the majority of gold and silver craftwork would have been in the hands of wealthy individuals or institutions: primarily aristocrats, the state or religious cults (especially Christianity from the fourth century onward). The gift of treasures, either special ex-votos or simply precious secular objects, in return for spiritual help was a prominent feature both of classical paganism and the Christianity that succeeded it. During the fourth century the great pagan temples were despoiled of their riches, much of which then came into the hands of the Church. Some items were remade into objects with explicitly Christian imagery and inscriptions, whilst others were simply accumulated. Votive vessels, except in extreme conditions such as the ransoming of prisoners, were legally inalienable. On a small scale this society can be seen in operation through the 56 objects known to have been donated to the church of St Sergios in the Syrian village of Kaper Koraon between 540 and 640 which were hidden at the time of Arab invasions. The prominence of dedi-

18 Justinian, San Vitale, Ravenna. The emperor brings an offering of a gold vessel to the altar

catory inscriptions even allows family trees of donors to be drawn up. Such practices of the endowment and accumulation of treasures in churches survived the downfall of the empire in the west, as can be seen by the example of the gift of treasures to churches by St Desiderius of Auxerre in seventh-century Francia.

Liturgical implements were of enormous importance in Christian cult. These items included ewers, ladles, strainers and spoons for the wine; plates, boxes and knives for the preparation of the host; fans to keep insects away; thuribles and lamps. The treasure lists included in the papal biographies that make up the *Liber Pontificalis* are a testament to the vast quantities of precious silver and gold vessels present by imperial or aristocratic gift in the great churches. Especially prominent in these inventories are all manner of light fittings which were designed to stand on the floor, to be fixed to the walls, or suspended from the ceiling. The expense of the oil required meant that a night-time display of light was itself a symbol of wealth and prestige. The resulting effect, with the precious metals glinting in the lamplight, was an important element in aristocratic and cultic life. The overall impact would have been magnified by the extensive use of silver and gilt for furniture revetments and in precious metal mosaics on the walls.

19 Justinian, San Vitale, Ravenna. Detail of the treasure gift

The receptacles for the body and blood of Christ, the chalice and paten, were of the highest status. Bearing in mind their sublime role of honour, it is not surprising that it was thought important that these vessels should be of a suitable magnificence. Finds of communion vessels are not uncommon: the Water Newton treasure is interpreted as being of this type. Early Byzantine examples could be plain, with inscriptions, or with complex figural scenes of Christ upon them, although it is only fair to point out that the ecclesiastical silver that survives is mostly from small village churches, and is thus likely to be of a modest nature compared with that in use at the great cathedrals.

A considerable number of late antique silver workshops are known from official stamps, including Antioch, Aquilea, Cologne, Constantinople, Heraclea, Mainz, Naissus, Nicomedia, Rome, Sirmium, Thessalonica and Trier. At each of these places, we can presume there to have been a substantial market for silver-ware. Pieces were distributed, sometimes by sale, but also by gift and exchange. However, there are very likely to have been several other centres which may or may not have used stamps. It must be recalled that we only have a tiny fraction of the original production in the period. These treasure items, after all, were bullion, and could be melted down by aristocrats in time of financial need, or indeed when fashion had changed and a new style was desired.

20 *San Vitale, Ravenna. The emperor's wife, Theodora, brings her offering*

The imperial jewellers were associated with the mint under the control of the Counts of the Sacred Largesses. The insignia of the Counts as shown in the *Notitia Dignitatum* includes belt buckles and brooches as well as coin. Thousands of items were distributed each year by the central government. From the fourth century, mint production was increasingly associated with the location of the court and craftsmen would frequently travel with the entourage as it passed from place to place. With the waning of the western empire, imperial patronage came to be centred firmly on Constantinople where silver began to be hallmarked at the end of the fourth century. With the decline in production at Antioch and Alexandria, Constantinople came to dominate silver and jewellery manufacture in the sixth and seventh centuries. Pieces were disseminated from there across and beyond the empire. The ancient world, especially the later Roman world, did not possess a highly developed market economy. Whilst local production and sale did take place, one explanation for the phenomenon of central production points to imperial patronage behind the process of gifts to retainers. Many items were then passed on as votives to local churches.

In both imperial and private workshops a variety of techniques, including casting, hammering, engraving, gilding and niello were employed. Stylistic

21 *San Vitale, Ravenna. Detail of Theodora's robe, showing the magi bringing gifts to the baby Jesus*

evidence, as well as that of makers' marks, other inscriptions and official quality stamps, can be employed to assign pieces to places or even to individual workshops. In the fourth and fifth centuries, aristocratic jewellery formed a similar style across the empire, with much use of filigree, and settings of pearls, amethysts and sapphires. The rise in the importance of gems and the decline in the care in gold-working are the main distinguishing features between late antique jewellery and that of the earlier empire. At the same time, craftsmen working around the localities and fringes of the Roman world were producing treasures in demotic styles variously influenced by the main aristocratic style of the central empire.

Silverware demonstrates that, alongside the rise of Christian motifs, secular taste continued to patronise traditional mythological motifs through into the seventh century. This is not to say, however, that this should be understood to demonstrate the persistence of pagan beliefs: the relevant imagery was probably enjoyed for its references to the rural idyll which remained prominent in late classical ideas of paradise. Elsner argues that the rise of allegorical ways of viewing in the Christian empire meant that the surface motif was often understood to represent something else: in other words, a plate with an apparently pagan scene could be understood as having a Christian

22 *Precious metal vessels glimmer amidst foliage, vault mosaics, Santa Constanza, early fourth century, Rome*

reference, whilst a Christian scene such as David fighting Goliath could be produced in association with early Byzantine imperial propaganda as referring to the holy struggle of the State against its enemies.

Treasure hoards are wonderful evidence for us, yet each must have represented a substantial loss for someone. It may seem like stating the obvious, but people do not lightly bury their treasure in the ground. It is clearly to be seen in many cases as an emergency act and an indication of a time of trouble. Moreover, the second obvious point to make is that the treasures we possess are the ones which were never recovered. There is a heavy concentration of hoards from the late Roman period, which, bearing in mind the chronic instability of many areas at the time, is hardly surprising. Treasures, as high-value easily portable goods, were premier targets for thieves and raiders including 'barbarians' or anyone else. The Church, however, as we shall see, was better able to protect its riches, because of respect for its sacrality. It is perhaps significant that liturgical pieces are rarely found in hoards, even though we know of their contemporary abundance through the evidence of our textual materials.

Holy wisdom

The Roman Empire had its origins in the third century BC and was to reach its greatest extent in the second century AD which was a time of peace and plenty. This stability was not to last. The third century saw a succession of bitter civil wars which triggered massive economic dislocation. The empire was brought back from the brink of dissolution by absolutist emperors such as Diocletian and Constantine. Their actions, however, brought only a temporary respite. The fifth century saw the break-up of the western half of the Roman empire leaving the east on its own. Under the great rulers of the sixth century, notably Justinian, the eastern empire staged a temporary recovery before retreating in the face of the devastating Arab expansion of the seventh century.

There is no single date when the Roman Empire ended and the Byzantine Empire began. These names are simply labels applied by modern historians indicating a shift towards an empire centred round the Greek east which shrank, gradually, over 1000 years, until there was little more than the city of Constantinople itself remaining. There was a great age of cathedral building across Europe in the high Middle Ages which followed a few slightly leaner early medieval centuries. The last great monument of the ancient world is often considered to be the sixth-century rebuilding of Constantine's church of Holy Wisdom (Hagia Sophia) in Byzantium.

Justinian 1 (AD 482-565), who ruled from 527, is also, arguably, the last of the great emperors with Roman, Europe-wide pretensions and goals. He attempted the reconquest of Italy, Spain and North Africa. He codified Roman law, had a scandalous marriage to the courtesan and actress Theodora which, as told by Procopios, could easily have graced the pages of Suetonius. Justinian also poured money into building works, both fortifications and churches, the greatest of which was Hagia Sophia. It was built in six years and was completed in 537. Its predecessor had been destroyed in city riots. Justinian needed to re-establish his authority, his control and his respect in the eye of God. The church is huge, measuring 77 by 79m and the impressive dome soared 50m above the floor and had a diameter of about 33m.

Procopios tells us that 'the Emperor, disregarding all questions of expense, eagerly pressed on to begin the work of construction, and began to gather all the artisans from the whole world'. Emphasis was placed, not only on the financial, but also on the engineering aspects of the construction:

> The upper part of this structure ends in the fourth part of a sphere, and above it another crescent-shaped structure rises, fitted to the adjoining parts of the building, marvellous in its grace, but by reason of the seeming insecurity of its composition, altogether terrifying. For it somehow seems to float in the air on no firm basis, but to be poised aloft to the peril of those inside it. Yet actually it is braced with exceptional firmness and security.

23 Justinian's great church of Hagia Sophia, Constantinople

Paul the Silentiary wrote a poem in praise of the building which brings to life the splendid decoration of the church which is now only preserved in fragments:

> Above all rises into the immeasurable air the great helmet [of the dome], which, bending over, like the radiant heavens, embraces the church. And at the highest part, at the crown, was depicted the cross, the protector of the city . . . Everywhere the walls glitter with wondrous designs, the stone for which came from the quarries of Proconnesus. The marbles are cut and joined like painted patterns, and in stones formed into squares or eight-sided figures the veins meet to form devices; and the stones show also the forms of living creatures. . .

85

A thousand lamps within the temple show their gleaming light, hanging aloft by long chains. Some lights are placed in the aisles, others in the centre or to east and west, or on the crowning walls, shedding the brightness of flame. Thus the night seems to flout the light of day, and be itself as rosy as the dawn . . .

So through the spaces of the great church come rays of light, expelling clouds of care, and filling the mind with joy. The sacred light cheers all: even the sailor guiding his ship on the waves, leaving behind him the unfriendly billows of the raging Pontus, and winding a sinuous course amidst creeks and rocks, with heart fearful at the dangers of his nightly wanderings – perhaps he has left the Aegean and guides his ship against adverse currents in the Hellespont, awaiting with taut forestay the onslaught of a storm from Africa – he does not guide his laden vessel by the light of the North Star, or the circling Bear, but by the divine light of the church itself. Yet not only does it guide the merchant at night, like the rays from the Pharos on the coast of Africa, but it also shows the way to the living God.

Gold mosaic decorated the dome whilst the silver revetments (of the lower walls and furniture) would, if 1mm thick, have taken 12,000lb of silver, or, if 3mm thick, 36,000lb. A later source lists a total of 600 persons assigned to serve in the church: 80 priests, 150 deacons, 40 deaconesses, 70 subdeacons, 160 readers, 25 chanters and 75 doorkeepers. The dome was damaged in an earthquake and had to be rebuilt in 563. The building has since become a mosque and been altered in various ways, but it remains one of the most astonishing attempts to blend physical form and Christian spirituality. Grand churches, in this age, had gone beyond being adjuncts of imperial grandeur. Their splendour, even if paid for by emperors, had surpassed that of the State's palaces. The State showed its power through the magnificence of its churches.

Part 2

This examines art and architecture at the geographical and chronological ends of empire: Britain and northern Gaul (northern France and Belgium) from the fourth to the sixth centuries. Classical art and architecture was embodied, in the fourth century, through grand churches, palaces and villas (country houses). As the political grip of the empire weakened local elites seem to have been less able or willing to spend their money on personal artistic and architectural display. In Britain, Roman rule ended *c.*410 in an atmosphere of chaos and revolt. The resulting vacuum of power was filled by invading Anglo-Saxons from 450 onwards. The south-west of Gaul was settled with Germanic Goths by the Roman government, whilst the rest was gradually conquered by various tribes, particularly the Franks. During all of this chaos and upheaval Churches remained the main centres for classical magnificence to an even greater extent than in Byzantium. Christianity had moved from the position of being the critic of Roman grandeur to becoming its chief exponent.

5 Stately homes

A line from W.H. Davies' most famous poem, 'a poor life this if, full of care, we have no time to stand and stare', is written on the base of his statue in the main shopping street in Newport in south Wales. His monument seemed to be ignored by the locals the day when I saw it. Perhaps familiarity breeds contempt, in which case what are we to make of the public statuary and grand buildings of the Roman world? Were the monuments of antiquity futile exercises in vanity? And who could have been their intended audience? This is a more complex question than it sounds because the privilege of standing and staring was just that – a privilege – in the ancient world. Just as the elite could govern and wheel and deal (*negotium*), so they had the resources which meant that they did not have to toil for their living. They could enjoy leisure and reflection, *otium*. One area in which the public and private life of aristocrats was mirrored was building schemes. These could be mainly for public impact through, for example, spending on town monuments. Or such spending could be more private, as in the construction of a palatial villa or 'stately home', the setting for leisure pursuits that would be appreciated together with one's friends and family. In the later empire the towns were declining as centres of patronage as their powers and revenues were sapped by central government, which is why I will be concentrating on the countryside. Part 2 of this book will look at the prestige of various aspects of the built environment and treasures in the world of the provincial elites at the geographical and chronological ends of the empire. It will be a case study in power and display, with a particular focus on the role of the Church in the transformation of Britain and Gaul from the fourth to sixth centuries.

The cultural history of the first few centuries AD in north-western Europe has often been studied in terms of 'Romanisation' followed by post-Roman 'Germanisation'. 'Romanisation' has traditionally been seen as the result of cultural choice. The key idea was expressed in Haverfield's *Romanisation of Roman Britain* which was written in the early twentieth century. The underlying paradigm was the superiority of Roman culture and, hence, its adoption by conquered peoples. This, however, has been criticised as being a product of colonial European ideas. Other recent notions include that of resistance to foreign cultures, or the idea that Roman-looking objects could be filled with local meanings or used in non-Roman ways. Overall, the idea behind this is relativism: that no culture is inherently superior. But the nature of Roman culture was also more complex than once realised. Moreover, there was a process of interaction and mutual influence between it and other cultures. The term 'Romanisation' is rather misleading in relation to such complexity.

Why should people change their own culture, art and lifestyles? The attitude of those with power must be of great importance. Economic capacity as controlled by political and social conditions would play its part. The elite occupies a position in our evidence from the ancient and medieval worlds which is greatly disproportionate to its numbers. This is because it is they who were able to use surplus wealth in cultural expressions such as art, architecture and literature. This means that when we study the characteristic culture of the Roman Empire, we are very often studying the culture of its upper classes.

Government policy would have played a prominent role in setting the cultural agenda through the favouring of nobility who were visibly in line with public ideology. The degree of order in public life would have affected the ability of the upper classes to collect the revenues from their estates and to spend as they might desire. A decline in economic prosperity and trade would badly affect the patronal abilities of the upper classes, whilst changes in government would have an impact upon many of the cultural choices of the landed classes who were ultimately at the mercy of military favour. The rise of the Church as an institution rivalling the cultural authority of governments must further be seen as an important factor in the differing cultural histories of Britain and northern Gaul in the fifth and sixth centuries.

This enquiry into the fate of late Roman art and architecture does not have the aim of lamenting their demise or to measure their standards against those of the succeeding early medieval culture, but simply to seek an explanation for the dramatic change in the nature of the built environment in north-western Europe during this period. Late Roman art and architecture can be seen, not just as subjects in isolation, but as components of antique material culture in a general sense. A division, however, may be made between the art and culture of ordinary Romans and that of their elite. The landed elite, together with the State and the Church, were the predominant builders and patrons in late antiquity. The Roman aristocracy's distinctive material culture was eloquently expressed through their patronage of public and religious buildings, as well as their mosaic- and marble-decorated villas and town houses. These reached a peak of magnificence in Britain and parts of Gaul in the fourth century. By the seventh century these traditions of building and decoration were virtually restricted to the Christian Church, and nobles apparently lived in simpler wooden dwellings.

How did this come about? In order to answer this question it is necessary to distinguish two linked phenomena, the first being changing economic circumstances and the second being changing cultural expectations. The traditional explanation has been that the late Roman civilian aristocracy would always have liked to maintain classical lifestyles and, therefore, that they only dropped these forms under the pressures of adversity. On the other hand, it is interesting to think of Peter Heather's explanation of the end of classical education for the secular elite in Gaul: this came about when learning in the old style was no longer advantageous in public careers. The assumption has often been that the collapse of much of Roman culture in Britain and Gaul occurred as a result of the end of Roman power in the region, an underlying assumption being that people would want to be Roman, and live and dress like Romans if only they could. This concept, however, ignores the fact that a major function of such material culture may have been to display a sense of belonging when that seemed empowering. The physical splendour of the Roman world was extremely expensive and such expenditure on display only made sense within the context of the system's smooth functioning.

Villas and aristocrats

The pleasures and prestige of *otium*, relaxation and contemplation, lent a powerful impetus to the building of grand country houses by the Roman elite. Building and decorating private residences on a large scale implies a long-term investment in property and suggests that processes of social competition were at work. Ostentatious villa-building, for example, was visible evidence of a claim to status by the owners and patrons. The advent of Romanised housing in the north-west of Europe took place in the context of the new reality of imperial power in the region from 50 BC onwards. Local aristocracies were becoming involved in the Romanised administration of their localities. Disarmed by the imperial armies these elites sought to assure their security by their place within the new Roman legal order. Building in a Romanised fashion advertised their participation in the new power structures to their patrons, rivals and subordinates. Tenants were thereby alerted to the social distance between themselves and their landlords who were taking on the physical appearance of the Romans. Disobedience to the landlord was foolhardy disobedience to Rome.

The construction of Roman-style country houses and farms is frequently viewed as a convenient indicator of 'Romanisation'. The value of this indicator should, of course, be tempered by an awareness of the extra costs of building on a grander scale than had hitherto been the case in the pre-Roman west and by the realisation that villa distribution must have been influenced by the productive capacity of the land. In the north of Britain villas are only prominent in the vale of York. In poor areas maybe the land could not bring sufficient returns on investment, hence there was little material Romanisation. Villas should be seen in their full social and economic context. Some early villas were built by veterans used to living in Roman-style accommodation. The many smaller ones were not the prerogative of the rich, but the spread of this building form should be understood in the contexts of fashion and emulation, as well as the generation and concentration of surplus wealth. Mark Gregson assembled a database of some 560 British villas. He saw the villa as the symptom of land being viewed as a commodity, associated with investment in property for its sale value. On the evidence of the rising number of villas in proportion to other forms of rural habitation, he concluded that there was a market economy developing, with buying and selling of land. Nevertheless, even at their peak, villas were but a tiny percentage of rural dwellings, just as the aristocracy was always vastly outnumbered by the peasantry.

We should not assume that all these houses were owner-occupied; some would have been rented out or run by bailiffs, or kept for the occasional visit of the owner. The situation was complex, raising important questions such as whether we think of villas as the central buildings on estates which were integrated into the Roman economic system. In fact many farms which must have been associated with market or taxation transactions were not built in a Romanised architectural style. There are some strange features, such as the lack of worker-housing near the main villa in many cases. Did workers live elsewhere, in villages perhaps? Or is this phenomenon simply down to incomplete excavations which ignored the surroundings of the main villa building? And to what extent were market exchanges or self-sufficiency prominent in different phases? Ausonius gives us a fascinating picture of his bailiff travelling through the fourth-century northern Gallic countryside bartering with other landowners for necessary goods. Such rare literary evidence is of great importance in understanding the later Roman countryside.

Villas were but one part of estates and many were far from ostentatious. Indeed the term itself is rather unsatisfactory, since it is sometimes applied to the main dwelling on an estate, and at other times to the main building complex including a range of agricultural structures. Moreover, it is important to note the trend over recent years to stress regional variation across the empire. A villa was not the same everywhere since there was a great variety of house forms, even within each small region. In Britain the usage is applied to country houses with Romanising features such as extensive use of masonry, plans based on right angles, presence of mosaic or painted plaster, and heating systems or baths. Greg Woolf, in his recent study of the rise of Roman Gaul, has written that we should think in terms of general cultural influences and fashions: 'The rebuilding of "native farms" as *villae* thus reflects a deep internalisation of Roman tastes, rather than a desire to imitate Roman style *in toto*' – in other words, not an explicit desire to assert Romanness by building identically to people in Italy, but rather to show status in a society heavily influenced by Roman standards. Romanness itself, of course, was never static. However, for centuries elite status was architecturally demonstrated in ways that had something of a common template, including such elements as mosaics, baths, tiled roofs and so forth. These traditions faltered at different dates in different regions, suggesting a variety of local circumstances.

Recent years have seen a rise in theoretical studies of the negotiating individual working out his or her options and acting not simply at the whim of circumstances and entrenched social structures. Large-scale house building was visible evidence of a claim to status by the builders within a social structure that valued such expressions, as was the case, for example, in early modern and modern England. When there are new foci of power in society – post-Roman royalty, for example – local elites may have been expected partly to appeal to traditional standards of prestige, but also to adopt to new conditions. The question is what material forms are equated with success and power at a particular point.

What was a provincial Roman aristocrat? There are many factors. Descent, wealth, culture, involvement in civic or imperial government, friendship links: all these played a part. Ammianus left us a famously satirical sketch of the towering pretensions and vulgar ostentation of the Roman senators: those who have money can be ridiculed easily for misusing it. What did aristocrats do? The answer, first and foremost, was that they owned and managed estates. They had the options of leisure or public life. They could maintain networks of friends through letters. They might have the time and education to enter the Church. They might serve at the royal court, or as ambassadors. And they might even make an attempt to become rulers themselves.

Arnheim argues that there was a steady revival of the western senatorial aristocracy from a low point under Diocletian. From Constantine onward large numbers of aristocrats were once more appointed to top imperial posts. He sees this situation as leading to the steady weakening of central government as a feature of the west and the consequent distribution of power amongst the aristocracy. The crowning of bureaucratic careers with senatorial rank boosted the order in the fourth century, whilst the eclipse, in the fifth-century west, of the imperial government left senators as dominant figures in many localities. Great estates can be seen as virtually self-contained and their owners enormously rich and powerful so long as their property was not endangered. One can point to suggestions of large-scale tax evasion amongst the topmost aristocracy as a basic example of the ability of local elites to defy the imperial government at this date. A law of 397 claimed that in some provinces only half the senatorial taxes had been paid. This phenomenon was coupled with poor people selling their property and perhaps themselves in exchange for noble protection. There is not an overwhelming amount of evidence, but we do have Salvian's testimony that people 'driven by fear of the enemy flee to the *castella* . . . give themselves over to the yoke of being *inquilini* [low-grade tenants, tied to service of their master].'

The head of a grand estate would start the day with a wash and a prayer to the Master of the Universe, before dealing with business matters prior to enjoying a lunch party, writing or hunting. The Roman 'paterfamilias' (head of the family) was *dominus* (lord) in his own household. Grand villas resembled palaces, as was the case with Piazza Armerina in Sicily, with its vast floor mosaics, a *triclinium* (dining hall) and large basilica, below the apse of which was an area marked out by coloured marble flooring that may well have been the place for a throne. This may have been the retreat for the emperor

Maximian on his abdication with Diocletian in 305; however, the imperial attribution is unproven and there is nothing to suggest that this building could not have been owned by any rich senator. The presence of audience halls points to nothing other than the fact that a great landowner was emperor on his estates, with his ancestors in official dress present in the house in statuary and painting. The hunt mosaics illustrate this at Piazza Armerina in that the men are shown in the official dress of authority of the Tetrarchic age. Despite the strenuous nature of hunting they wear the external manifestation of power. Clothing and protocol was crucial in social definition. The 'lord' is shown in the North African mosaic of Dominus Julius, seated, virtually enthroned, opposite his wife who is being offered a necklace from her jewel-box by an attendant. In his personal audience hall a late Roman aristocrat could approximate before his guests the transcendent remoteness of the emperor himself. There is no evidence of a different style of life between pagan and Christian aristocrats in the fourth century.

Senatores do appear very late in our sources. They turn up, for example, in the late sixth-century *Histories* of Gregory of Tours. Who were they? Strictly speaking the senatorial classes were the elites of Rome and Constantinople. In practice many rarely went to the capitals and many others would have had land scattered across the empire. Melania, a lady of senatorial family with an income of 120,000 *solidi*, had lands across Italy, Sicily, Spain and Africa, and had rather more income than the prominent Italian senator Symmachus, who could still mention in his letters three houses in Rome and 15 villas in Italy. Yet it appears that they were both outside the topmost rank of aristocratic incomes of the time. Gregory's senators may have represented the direct descendants of ancient noble families, or they may simply have been substantial landowners in the late Roman style. That style of elitism demanded time and money in the projection of a specific image through spending on art and architecture. The vanishing of senators from later French evidence may indicate the end of a lifestyle.

Villas in Britain

As with the patterns of urban life, building forms in the countryside varied widely across western Europe. Whilst British evidence shows a crash around the early fifth century, and this appears to accord with the end of Roman control, the Ager Veientanus survey north-east of Rome found a serious reduction in rural occupation in the third century, but no further such crisis until the sixth century. By contrast, a major survey in Etruria identified continuous decline from 200 to 500, by which time 50-80 per cent of rural sites had been abandoned. In Britain, villa numbers peaked at around 330. Bearing in mind the Italian evidence just mentioned, the great abandonment of towns and villas at the end of Roman Britain should be seen in the light of greater discontinuity but simply as the end of Roman rule. This is not to deny the importance of a state component, merely to say that this must have been only one part of the equation.

To give the British evidence in more detail: Celtic-style round-houses and villages continue throughout the Roman period, with slowly rising numbers of Romanised villa dwellings. These show some stagnation in the third century, then a peak in numbers, size and decoration in the early fourth followed by a steady fall from then on. This gradual development was due both to the pace of acculturation and to the generational agglomeration of landholdings which provided sufficient surplus for substantial building works. Only at Fishbourne, Angmering and Eccles are mosaics and bath buildings known from villas in the first century. Only seven villas contain substantial second-century mosaics: Fishbourne, Sussex; Boxmoor and Park St, Herts; High Wycombe and Latimer, Bucks; Well, Yorks and Winterton, Lincs. To quote from Frere, 'the vast majority of villa-mosaics, like the wealthy villas that they adorned, are characteristic of the fourth century in Britain'. Before then Roman-style display appears to have gone more into town houses and urban public building.

The last great rise of confidence in Roman art in Britain was expressed in the early fourth-century embellishments of the great villas, such as floor mosaics. The high point of this art arrives in 300–350, with almost half the examples coming from Gloucestershire, Somerset and Dorset. Some of the most flourishing workshops were in Cirencester (examples at Chedworth, North Leigh and Newton St Loe). Another workshop was based at Dorchester (Frampton, Hinton St Mary, Mow Ham and Lufton). Another was in the north, centred perhaps on York (Winterton, Brantingham, Horkstow, Rudston). Examples of this art include the vast (2500ft^2) floor at Woodchester, perhaps the largest north of the Alps, which was an Orpheus pavement set in a reception room, showing the power of gods over nature as a metaphor for the power of the owner over his land. At Hinton St Mary, meanwhile, we find the famous pavement with a bust with Chi Rho and pomegranate, a symbol of eternity.

The fourth century sees the grandest villas, but with a growing disparity between a few rich ones and the rest. We should note the sophisticated designs of some villas, such as Littlecote with its grand gatehouse dated *c*.360, and Woodchester, which was laid out around three huge courts and possessed a massive triclinium which needed four pillars to hold up the roof over the previously mentioned mosaic. The inner court was residential, whilst the outer courts were for business and included the estate manager's house and farm buildings. Another grand villa, Castle Copse, Wiltshire, was, at 100m^2, larger than Woodchester. The quality of Castle Copse's construction places this building amongst the most palatial in Britain and makes it comparable with the finest in the empire. Britain was clearly not a backwater in such designs.

However, the overwhelming majority of people continued to live in huts or cottages. The villas were merely one element within a landscape still dominated by traditional architecture. Up to a dozen or so really grand palaces date from that last great age of Roman aristocratic prosperity. The number of villas rose until the early fourth century, but their average size fell from the mid-second century. What we can see is the spread of Roman-style houses through a wider range of the social spectrum down to lower levels who could not afford a large dwelling. In the late fourth century both the average size and the overall number of inhabited villas was then falling. Not only that but standards of maintenance plummeted, with what is identified as 'squatter occupation' spreading from 350 onwards, well before the end of Roman control.

When we bear in mind the rise of the palace villas, the picture is one of increasing social polarisation, which is remarkable because earlier Roman society had already been divided between the very rich few and the very many poor. This accentuation is something that was found across the Roman empire. It seems that the most powerful people had enough clout at court to avoid many duties and taxes and, therefore, rose further in wealth. Also, across the empire, the position of the majority of the population appears to have been deteriorating. Why? Taxes were rising (the army was doubled in size in the early fourth century). State exactions had always fallen disproportionately on the poor in the Roman world, since the taxation system was not designed to be progressive. It seems that the poor were being forced into ever greater dependency on landlords. In other words, if a poor freeman could not pay his taxes, he could escape from the situation only by passing the burden onto his patron or landlord who would gain recompense by services in kind. The status of many people, so-called *coloni*, who had previously been poor but free, now appears to have slipped into something akin to medieval serfdom.

A good example of the fate of villas in Britain, and one where the history of the building has been carefully charted, is Barnsley Park, where a winged-corridor villa was built between 360 and 375. In the late fourth century the residential quarters were used as part of the working farm, and around 400 the roof and walls were demolished down to the lowest five courses of masonry. Farm life continued and the old stone was carted away, with final abandonment occurring some time in the fifth century. The main house was not huge by villa standards, but it was enormous when compared with the other farm buildings. The last villa mosaics and the latest villas cluster round Bath, Gloucester and the Cotswolds, in what has been referred to as a 'sheltered' region. An example is Hucclecote, where coins in mortar bedding give a date for a mosaic floor of 395 or later. The end of this art is clearly associated with the end of the villas and should be seen in the light of dramatic change in the nature of the secular architecture of the time.

Gildas, a post-Roman British writer, talked of the destruction of towns, but he makes no mention of villas. Did he not know about them? Villas seem to have gradually decayed, the grand buildings being demolished to make way for something more utilitarian like animal pens. At many sites there was a distinct phase of occupation from the second half of the fourth century, involving the cutting of hearths through fine floors and the abandonment of parts of the buildings. For example, at Haddon in Cambridgeshire the bath house went out of use in the late fourth century. It was partly demolished, but the east wall still stood and a mill and corn dryer were installed in a wooden extension. At Castle Copse mosaics were roughly patched and then obliterated as industrial activity moved into residential areas and timber construction replaced masonry.

The villas vanish from the archaeological record in the fifth and sixth centuries, although one may wonder at a literary reference, such as that in St Patrick's letters to a 'villula' (little villa): could this, by any chance, be a high-status place, the word a product of modesty? But from the archaeological evidence it would seem that the villa tradition was not maintained. British society did maintain certain prestigious centres, as can been seen from the case study by Alcock of Dinas Powys, Glamorgan: a hall and defensive enclosure occupied from the fifth to the eighth centuries. Lines of eaves-drip have been identified, giving the outlines of buildings (one such being perhaps 15 by 8m) which do not otherwise appear since they were frame-built rather than post-built (i.e. with uprights that went into long beams that lay along the ground). This site was probably a chief's residence.

A similar site is Cadbury hillfort, with its post-Roman post-hole rectilinear building, 19m long by 10m wide, which was three-quarters of the floor area of the largest hall at the exceptional Anglo-Saxon site of Yeavering. A timber rampart shows a south-west gate structure which, perhaps due to 'excavation strategies' elsewhere, is currently unparalleled in Britain other than at Dinas Powys. Building on such a scale is exceptional in the post-Roman period and the focus on reuse of Iron Age defensive sites is interesting. The fifth-century British hillforts find equivalents on the Continent where a number of hilltop retreats appear to have been maintained, although French opinion associates them typically with times of emergency rather than permanent elite residence. Villas are suggested, by the French archaeologist Van Ossel, to have persisted as the place of normal habitation at the foot of hills in parts of northern Gaul.

The fifth century in Britain and large areas of Gaul saw not just cultural change, but, to quote David Miles, 'there is no doubt . . . a substantial economic and probably demographic collapse'. British villa construction ground to a halt in the late fourth and early fifth centuries, no doubt in association with a decline in the availability of specialist labour and resources and perhaps with the end of the coin-based market economy. And since most villas were at the core of estates, we may wonder at the extent of a crisis in agriculture and revolutions in landholding. The severing of ties with overseas landlords may have been a significant factor. Land confiscated in the aftermath of unsuccessful British-based attempts at the imperial throne may have been granted by the emperor to people who never visited the province, leading to an absentee landholding class and a vacuum of ownership when Britain was finally sundered from the empire.

We cannot expect to find in post-Roman Britain the same concentration of wealth as had occurred under the Roman period of property stabilisation. It will seem to us a materially poor culture, a poverty that only becomes mysterious when we compare it with the examples we do possess of Anglo-Saxon magnificence which came from a society with an apparently similar level of social organisation. Post-Roman British aristocrats are hard to spot archaeologically. Perhaps feasting their retinues was very important for the British elite: this would not leave much trace. Such people may have continued, at least for a while, to think of themselves as Romans, but their culture, simply through its comparative invisibility, was not classical. This does not necessarily mean that we are looking at a Celtic revival of pre-Roman traditions, since Greg Woolf has argued that the evidence points to a 'forget-fulness' of the ancient past in the Celtic provinces of the empire. This is in direct contradiction to the view expressed most forcibly by Hunter-Mann, that 'the Romano-British socio-economic system was essentially the LPRIA [late pre-Roman Iron Age] system with "Roman" embellishments'. It is best to conclude that post-Roman Britain was in some ways similar in appearance to its pre-Roman predecessor.

Villas in Gaul

Gaul presents us with more evidence than Britain, both literary and archaeo-logical. 'Ville' in French comes from 'villa'. We have 'village' in English, but 'villa' was used in later Anglo-Saxon as equivalent to 'vicus' (small trading settlement). Since 'villa' does not appear in early place names, unlike a 'wic' element derived from 'vicus', it seems clear that at the time of the settlements the newcomers found things called 'vici' but not 'villae' and that the latter word came to be applied to the former. By contrast, various French place name endings, such as -ac, -ecque, -gnan and -gny, have been described as obviously derived from the adjectival forms of the names of the former Gallo-Roman proprietors of estates. No such thing occurs in England. Beyond this general picture of Gallic continuity the varied fate of the villas and their art across Gaul can easily be seen from the fact that in Aquitaine there was strong continuity into the fifth century, whilst in Gallia Belgica mosaic art is very rare in the fourth century, never having recovered from the third century. The exception in the region is the Mosel valley along to Cologne and Trier which was the then centre of imperial power in the north.

Villas were rising in splendour in the region of fourth- and fifth-century Bordeaux, with repairs and additions after a third-century slump. The city itself was, from the evidence of excavations, of great prosperity. The walls did not define the edge of the thickly inhabited area, whilst all available space within, including areas previously uninhabited, was fully exploited. There was apparently no room for an intramural cathedral until the sixth century. The city was a major centre for pottery production and trade. Mosaic datings are interesting: the peak in Aquitaine comes in the fourth and fifth centuries. The mosaic workshops there seem to have been functioning well into the sixth century and perhaps later. Although there are some sixth-century mosaics from outside Aquitaine, for instance at Fondettes, examples from the north are very infrequent. Nevertheless, even in south-west Gaul there seem to have been declining numbers of senators, and the patrons of many of the mosaics and other art works may have been of Germanic origin. There is no reason to believe that these architectural and art styles can only have been employed by 'Romans'.

If we move to the mid-fifth century we can turn to the letters and poems of Sidonius Apollinaris, born in 431 or 432, prefect of Rome in 468 and bishop of Clermont in 470. Sidonius' writing is in the heavy late antique style. He did not see an opposition between pagan classicism and Christian culture, but between civilisation and barbarism. Classical culture needed to be maintained lest one should become barbarian in attitude of mind. At the same time he had to steer a pragmatic course in a world of rapid change. He wrote with perhaps a shade of sarcasm to Syagrius, the 'new Solon of the Germanic Burgundians', who had learnt the barbarian tongue. The publication of Sidonius' works was a Roman aristocratic act. Theses texts were expected to circulate amongst his friends. He knew well both the imperial and Gothic courts. Nevertheless, the picture presented by Sidonius of the Gothic king, Theodoric, was very much reminiscent of a Roman ruler. His days were spent in prayer, gaming, hunting, hearing petitions and business, then closing with a supper party accompanied by soothing music. This picture may have been intended to make the king seem more culturally acceptable as an overlord. Sidonius was clinging to ancient modes of prestige which continued, for a while, to hold considerable sway with those in power (in southern Gaul at least), or so one would believe from reading him.

Great villas were a classical quintessence. Sidonius presents us with idealised depictions, as in the example of Consentius, who had a town house and a suburban estate, the villa on which was praised for its symmetry, chapel, colonnades and baths, views over lush countryside, store rooms and stock of books. A similar picture of tranquillity and abundance appears in the description of Sidonius' own Avitacum (influenced by Pliny's descriptions of two of his villas), as well as his accounts of the villas of Apollinaris and Tonantius Ferroleus at Vorocingus and Prusianum on the way to Nimes. The idea of these texts was to convey an image of prosperity, but it is clear that in many areas the fifth century was much harder going than the fourth. This was an age in which virtue could be made of moderation, as in Paulinus of Pella's family's meagre silverware, and the lack of painted plaster at Avitacum. There was prosperity in Bordeaux, perhaps indicating that the Gothic kingdom kept better order than existed in the disputed zones between kingdoms. Overall, in Gaul there are far fewer sites in good repair in the fifth than the fourth century. Even in Aquitaine, such wealthy sites as Séviac, Saint-Séver, Sarbazon, Orbessan and Sorde-l'Abbeye do not argue for more than the survival of a narrowing Romanised elite.

Two fragments of Sidonius' epitaph survive, and the reconstructed inscription celebrates both the episcopal and the Roman glory of the bishop. In most cases Sidonius' attitudes and style encourage the reader to see continuity where there may have been disruption. His *Romanitas* was not universal. He was exceptional in that he had long been involved in imperial service. Each summer from 471 to 475, Clermont was besieged by Goths keen to expand their kingdom. Sidonius, returning from Rome, knew how weak the western empire was. Outside the walls houses were burnt and inside people starved. The inhabitants raised their own small forces and received the aid of the Burgundians who did not want any further Gothic expansion. Many Catholic sees were vacant in the heretical Arian Gothic kingdom. The defence of Clermont was interwoven with the defence of orthodox Christianity. The city was finally surrendered in a treaty and Sidonius was packed off into exile to a fortress near Carcassonne where he had to listen through the night to drunken Gothic women arguing. However, Sidonius was finally to return and co-operate with the Gothic king's count, Victorius, who was soon a patron of the Church there.

The image of landed elites as embattled can be derived from references to fortification which appear in Gallic texts: in Sidonius' description of the refuge Burgus Pontus Leontius, as well as in the hybrid buildings, praised by Venantius Fortunatus, which formed the citadel of Nicetius, bishop of Trier, *c.*525-66. This castle was a 'magnificent palace' and 'the house itself formed a kind of fortress', with marble pillars, a chapel, a double ballista 'whence projectiles could fly forth spreading death and havoc in their course', water flowed, and vines and orchards fruited. A study of late antique North African mosaics has shown that towers and high walls were consistent features of the depiction of villas there. However, the degree to which many of these architectural features were practical or designed for style in the context of the prestige of imperial fortifications is unclear.

A comparison between Fortunatus' sixth-century poems describing the Moselle, and Ausonius' fourth-century *Mosella*, is instructive. The same peaceful and fruitful landscape delights the eye, but the villas have vanished from the later account along with mythological references. Nicetius' castle was not only able to survive courtesy of its walls, but probably also because its episcopal possessor had installed protective relics there since the tower was 'a place of the holy things'. It was, therefore, much less like a villa than like a miniature early medieval town.

However, most villas fail to show evidence of destruction but rather of an end of investment in building and rebuilding. The traditional explanation is that this was due to lack of resources, but, as I will show, churches could still be funded, or, at one remove, gifts of land made which provided surplus allowing bishops to build. There was, however, a reduction in the concentration of resources, thus minimising the level of competition and removing the grand villa as a sine qua non of respectability. The traditional French archaeologists' explanation, that persisting villas are hidden under modern towns since they became villages in the Middle Ages, is convenient, but does not explain the differential pattern between northern and southern Gaul, and the vanishing of villas from texts. We do not have to suggest that the villa owners all fled. Perhaps it was more effective, in unsettled areas, to spend in new ways which were more useful in cementing social bonds?

6 Power and treasure

The last chapter ranged across the north-west of Europe, from the fourth to the sixth centuries, the period of the end of the empire in that region. This chapter focuses on a specific case study in discontinuity in the use of physical splendour. The *Anglo-Saxon Chronicle*, half a millennium after the supposed events, gave as the entry for 418 that 'in this year the Romans collected all the treasures which were in Britain, and hid some in the ground, so that no one could find them afterwards, and took some with them into Gaul'. Academic fashion has changed since Haverfield, in the first substantial study of 'Romanisation' in Britain, wrote of the fifth century and the coming of the Anglo-Saxons: 'during the long series of disasters, many of the Romanised inhabitants of the lowlands must have perished. Many must have fallen into slavery, and may also have been sold into foreign lands. The remnant, such as it was, doubtless retired to the west.' It is now recognised that the Germanic invaders were far fewer in number than once had been assumed and that their arrival largely post-dated the collapse of Romanised life in Britain. This realisation should be seen in the context of a powerful academic impetus to emphasise 'continuity' from Rome to the Middle Ages. However, it is possible that recent attempts to identify the achievements of British culture in the post-Roman period (which even extend to the contention that there may have been a minor economic boom with the removal of imperial taxation) underestimate the potential for disorder in the sudden absence of Roman military control.

It is in this historical context that a recent survey by Hobbs, showing the proportion of British to Continental finds of late fourth- to early fifth-century silver-plate hoards in Western Europe to be almost 50 per cent, will be viewed. This period is also a dramatically high point for depositions of coins, both on their own and together with other objects. The years 395-411 saw a quarter of all the precious-metal hoards from Britain, a quantity that is only exceeded by the political and economic crisis years 260-75, when a third of the hoards were deposited. The earlier period, however, saw extensive abandonment of debased issues of coinage, whilst the latter involved loss of high value objects and coin issues. Whilst coinage is also found sporadically, most of the surviving treasure objects are the result of the retrieval of buried hoards in recent years. Waves of hoards are evidence for the interruption of the circulation pattern. Study of precious-metal deposits across Europe shows a characteristic set of results. Finds are minimal across Europe except 238-60 along the Rhine and Danube, from 260-75 in central and northern Gaul and lowland Britain, from 275-96 in Britain (during the British separation from central authority), and from 395-411 in lowland Britain. The third century shows a wide spectrum of hoards, including bronze, showing deposition by poorer people. There are fewer late low-value hoards. Were the middle-ranking people impoverished later? Or was it only then that the elite was threatened?

These periods correspond to waves of political and economic upheaval, but many other foci of change do not seem to have produced such a rash of precious-metal hoards. Hoarding in the ground will vary according to accepted social custom, but the non-recovery of such accumulations will not, save in the case of votive hoards, which most of these are unlikely to have been. The comparative scarcity of finds from the early Middle Ages (the survey generally excludes burials with jewellery) is particularly intriguing. But if a wave of hoards indicates a dislocation in circulation then we would not expect to find this in the period of the Germanic migrations, of the fourth to sixth centuries, which saw increased redistribution of precious metal objects.

Depeyrot has commented that the Merovingian (early medieval French) economy was largely one of pillage: 'seizing treasures and land was the principal activity of Merovingian armies'. If the post-Roman period of raiding is considered as a functioning social system, it is the years of the break with the previous period of social stability which would be expected to produce clusters of evidence. The Roman period clearly saw temporary dislocations, followed by the re-imposition of the imperial pattern. In Britain, as we have seen above, the Roman system was rudely interrupted in the early fifth century, whilst in most of Gaul it slowly evolved: this fits nicely with the evidence of precious metal finds.

Defined as hidden collections of valuable objects primarily of gold and silver, hoards of treasure arouse as great an interest today as they did in the Middle Ages, as can be seen from the press reaction to one of the most recent and significant assemblages, the Hoxne treasure from Suffolk, with its wealth of precious metal objects placed into a box that was then packed with coins. Newspaper coverage of the Hoxne find centred closely upon the excitement of the finders and the value of the hoard. One article included an image of a giant coin with a map of Britain set in it and a list of the sale values of various recent ancient treasures. Judith Plouviez, from Suffolk County Council, enthused that the find was 'priceless in terms of the knowledge it will give us', but the public excitement was over the monetary value of the collection, which, it was speculated, could be as much as £10,000,000.

How can we go beyond generalised enthusiasm at these finds and bring the social realities of abandoned treasures back to life? It is hard to strike a balance between overdramatising and sanitising the past. The discovery of mutilated skulls at Caistor-by-Norwich was publicised by the press as being evidence for a gruesome massacre at the end of the Roman period. Archaeologists now suggest that the damage to the bones is more likely to have been the result of plough damage to skulls. On the other hand it is hard to imagine that the fifth century was a period of peaceful transition.

A recent edition of *The Guardian* newspaper reported the story of a peasant woman in the village of Jusici in eastern Bosnia, who, with her husband, had concealed all their valuables:

> Hanifa Islamovic was on her hands and knees, clawing soil from a three foot hole. She was red-faced and desperate. 'It was here, we buried it right here.' There was a frantic edge to her voice . . . amid the rubble of her gutted house, Mrs Islamovic had found Hamed's [her husband] green anorak and a pair of rubber boots, encrusted with dried blood. One wall of the house was spattered with dried blood. 'They must have tortured him until he told them where our money was buried', Mrs Islamovic said. The widow, aged 58, had cleaned Hamed's coat and wore it to keep off the rain.
> (Borger, 30 September 1996)

We lack such convenient sources as this report, or indeed the diary of Samuel Pepys, which recorded the hiding of a hundred crowns in his garden by his wife at a time when the Dutch fleet was menacing London and her husband's political future was in doubt. The danger passed and the diarist was able, with much delay and cursing, to find some of the coins. As Bradley asks, discussing this example, would we have correctly understood this deposition without the contemporary account? The task, therefore, is a challenging one. This is not to say that it is impossible. We can try to compare assemblages with other hoards of the time, creating a chronological and geographical context for each find. More specifically we can compare deposition occurrence with degradation or destruction at nearby villas in the light of the overall continuation (or otherwise) of the local archaeological record. In much of the Roman west the picture is one of repeated disturbance and occasional destruction, whilst in Britain the picture is of a sudden and spectacular economic collapse in the early fifth century, meaning, presumably, the end of the old Romanised aristocratic lifestyle. Deposition of treasures is further represented in the pillage hoards of Scotland and Ireland, before the spread of Germanic culture saw the placing of substantial amounts of jewellery in graves. The wave of hoards from c.390–420 seems to indicate a different sort of change from that which happened with barbarian settlement. Where there is a relative absence of evidence from post-Roman Britain, as occurs after the wave of late fourth- and early fifth-century depositions, does that mean there was peace? On the evidence of the post-Roman British writer Gildas, surely not. If he is to be trusted there was slaughter. And thefts that kept the gold and silver circulating.

State power and authority were intended to be used in the late Empire to maintain stability, to ensure that wealth circulated from the landowners to the treasury, out to the army and back again. There was no abrupt division between gift transactions under the empire and pay in gold or silver coin. And there was no abrupt division between Roman monetary exchange and post-

24   Silver vessel, missorium, *showing the emperor Theodosius enthroned, probably made as a state gift, late fourth century.* Real Acad. de la Historia, Madrid

Roman treasure gifts. Indeed, early medieval offerings of treasure have been seen as a 'final flowering' of the Roman tradition of imperial largesses which were to be superseded by gifts of estates by the central Middle Ages. Whilst the Romans promoted a huge circulation of gold and silver, much of it in coin, it must be emphasised that Roman gold coinage was itself 'special-purpose money', associated with state and military organisation, being of far too great a value for everyday transactions. From the end of the fourth century, as we have seen, the copper coinage progressively collapsed across much of Europe. What validated the Roman gold coinage appears, therefore, not to have been the state, but the gold. The Counts of the Sacred Largesses were in charge of issuing both currency and jewelled insignia. Coins, along with jewellery items and dishes, were given out by the State as gifts to barbarian kings, servants and soldiers according to rank and honour. Crisis for the empire came when warriors found that they could get more treasure, and hence wealth and status, and, therefore, power, by going independent than they could in handouts from the state.

We should distinguish between the use of treasure within the empire by the government and its employment by private individuals. In the world of the late Roman aristocracy treasures took the form of jewellery and other items of costume, tableware, vessels and general furnishings. Gold and jewels were applied to items as diverse as books, swords, chairs, bridles, carriages and cloaks, more for personal display rather than simply for hoarding. Silver tableware was one of the most characteristic treasure forms of the period. Much recent debate has fastened on the issue of how important the recently excavated silver treasures were in terms of contemporary levels of wealth. Great surviving treasures are, in fact, in Roman and medieval terms, rather small collections of material, if the figures from such lists of those to be found in the *Liber Pontificalis* (biographies of the Popes) may be trusted. By and large, it may be guessed that we have, perhaps, been overawed by these surviving collections, which form a large part of surviving late- and post-classical silver, but yet must represent a tiny part of what once existed.

Treasure transactions crossed from secular to religious life through the medium of votive offerings, that is gifts to God or to the gods, some of which took the form of depositions in the ground. These were offered half in pride and half in fear and hope, although the official Christian line was that when someone offers property to God, 'let him not offer it with the boldness of one who gives a gift. Let him offer his gift not with the confidence of buying redemption, but with the duty of supplication.' Wealth was passing steadily away from pagan cults. The Thetford treasure has been seen as a pagan cult hoard, hidden against persecution. The Church was to become further enmeshed in the treasure society of the early Middle Ages when, by the later seventh century, it started to take grave goods rather than let them go into the burial. The survivals of silver from village churches in Syria demonstrates that treasures were present in even apparently very minor Christian centres in the late classical and early medieval worlds.

Roman aristocratic society was based on a high degree of social snobbery, such that refinement could be praised above sheer display. Silverware was used by individuals as sophisticated pictures for display. Paulinus of Pella noted that amongst the appurtenances of the attractive household of his earlier years he possessed 'silverware of greater worth than weight', and Sidonius Apollinaris, aping earlier attitudes, protested modestly on inviting a friend to a banquet that 'our salvers are only modest and not so made that their artistry atones for their weight'. Plates were not simply viewed for their bullion value, which was of course highly important, but also as art objects in their own right.

Such images of aesthetic appreciation can be set against the 'barbaric' desire of raiders for the maximum quantity of riches. Booty was often divided up and retained almost as a form of coinage. Perhaps the most famous 'hacksilver' hoard to have been found in Britain came to light on the crown of the hillfort at Traprain Law, 20 miles east of Edinburgh, where there was no evidence of 'Roman style' occupation. This large hoard consisted of myriad items most of which had been flattened and broken using hammers and axe blows. The excavation report talked of the 'barbaric treatment that it [the silverware] had received at the hands of its last possessors'. It was concluded that 'the collection seems to include an assortment of plate gathered together either in a series of raids or in a single raid which has been extensive'. From coin evidence the date of deposition is likely to have been the first half of the fifth century. Many items from the hoard were chopped in two with only one half being found in the assemblage, indicating that division had already taken place. Other notable 'hacksilver' treasures from the British Isles are from Balinrees and Balline in Ireland, both of which consisted of a wide variety of broken plate and ingots bearing apparently official inscriptions. These hoards include the last issues to be present in Britain, and deposition is dated to the period *c.*420-60, in other words well after the end of Roman control in Britain.

Gregory of Tours tells a famous story of the turbulent society of later fifth-century Gaul, when the Roman Syagrius, dwelling in Soissons, was defeated by Clovis, king of the Franks, whose followers subsequently pillaged the churches of the city making off with many metal treasures. The bishop requested the return of a particular ewer and, in order to allow this, Clovis claimed the item even though he was only entitled to a share of the plunder. One soldier, however, 'raised his axe and struck the ewer. "You shall have none of this booty," he cried, "beyond your fair share"'. But the king handed the smashed vessel over to the bishop's envoy and, on a later occasion, split open the soldier's skull saying, 'this is what you did to my ewer at Soissons'!

It was once thought that 'hacksilver' hoards always represented the brutal spoils of victory. However, it has been argued that the occasional presence of neat parcels of scrap of specific weights, together with the appearance of ingots, shows that certain treasures represented federate payments. Such packets of folded silver and other items have been found from Roman Britain. At Whorlton in Yorkshire in 1810, there were brought to light several hundred silver coins, combined with silver objects and bars, including broken and folded sheet silver. The hoard is paralleled, albeit on a far smaller scale, by the treasure-trove found at Water Newton in 1974, which consisted of a leather purse holding 30 *solidi*, with two pieces of folded silver, all hidden inside a pottery bowl with a bronze lid as a cover. The two packets weighed 321g and 642g, roughly one and two pounds of silver. The point is clear: that whether in the form of imperial donatives, or in private exchanges, scrap and bullion could be used as a form of currency in this period.

Both Romans and 'barbarians' viewed gold and silver ultimately as bullion. Yet while the former may have held specific attitudes towards style and refinement, this should not lead us to believe that 'barbarians' were uninterested in issues of design. They possessed their own remarkable metalworking traditions. Remaking of vessels in the latest style was practised in both Roman and post-Roman society. The phenomenon of bracteates, thin metal discs based on Roman coins which were worn round the neck, suggests the enthusiasm of Germanic aristocrats to emulate Roman precious-metal coin designs for their aesthetic, or perhaps amuletic, value, but not surely as badges of loyalty to the empire, which was the purpose of the original design. As Axboe and Kromann wrote with reference to bracteates, 'the barbarians in Scandinavia knew and understood the Roman prototypes, and they borrowed only those features which fitted their world and their notions'.

Roman prestige goods had long been desirable beyond the imperial frontiers. Venantius Fortunatus, 'educated in Ravenna in a rhetorical tradition that placed a premium on an ornate and allusive classicism', found an admiring market for his verse amongst both Romans and Franks. His claim, 'let others give gifts of gold and gems to kings: it is words that you shall receive from poor Fortunatus', indicates a literary conceit understood by both peoples. Yet we cannot assume that all the newcomers were equally admiring, or be sure how much skill and discernment they would have had in relating to old standards. Classical precedents were often admired and sometimes adopted. What is to be envisaged is a selective use and enjoyment of Roman motifs and practices.

Forms of personal display did evolve, away from plate toward weaponry and jewellery, for example, as did mechanisms of transfer, away from written grants toward oral gifts. However, state treasure-hoards were important both in the world of the earlier Roman emperors and of Gregory of Tours. There was a continued importance of treasures in rewarding followers in Carolingian Francia despite abundant coinage. Charlemagne's huge treasure-hoard was at once a proof of his authority and a means of wielding it. Treasures circulated as they had previously, with a proportion being withdrawn into collections or in the form of religious votive offerings. The practices of treasure accumulation of the Roman state and of early medieval society might be said to be similar in many ways, albeit with the proviso that treasure objects and personal transactions rose in importance, whilst coinage, taxation and economic transactions declined (at least until the new silver issues of the seventh and eighth centuries). Roman society and 'barbarian' early medieval societies were mostly able to articulate the circulation of valuables. Not only barbarians raided: in one episode, the son of emperor Constantine III attacked relatives of emperor Honorius in Spain, took their estates and settled down, acting like just another rogue warlord. Above all, we should note that Romans and non-Romans were well used to employing treasure in the form of precious metal as bullion in negotiations with one another. As the Romans lost power so they also lost wealth through forced gifts and thefts, but the circulation system itself on much of the Continent was not disrupted. Something different, however, appears to have taken place in Britain between the withdrawal of imperial control and the settlement of the Anglo-Saxons.

A vacuum of power

There was, therefore, substantial continuity in the importance and employment of treasures beyond the Roman period across much of the west. Christianisation had no major effect in disrupting the social importance of gold and silver save that offerings, which might once have gone to temples, now went to churches. A wave of unclaimed treasures in Britain indicates the localised failure of a system that otherwise kept treasures on display or circulating in society from late antiquity to the Middle Ages. The owners of substantial table silver would have been prosperous landowners and high-ranking military and civilian officials. Such items would not normally be buried, but passed on, sold or inherited and certainly not thrown away. Certain hoards surely may represent some sort of catastrophe. The Kaiseraugst treasure was buried at the same time as three 'modest' deposits of bronze coins in the face of an immediate danger. With the Alemmanic invasions the treasures were not recovered, and the fortress where they were buried was, we must assume, stormed. However, bearing in mind the rarity of finds from the Continent in the fifth century, most treasure there seems to have been transferred to the newcomers rather than hidden in the ground. It may be that some was simply looted, but much else is likely to have been offered up through negotiation since there were substantial figures in authority to placate. If this were not so, and theft and death were indeed widespread, it would be hard to understand the paucity of hoards in Gaul. It seems that little treasure was placed in the ground and left there, perhaps because it could be used as a bargaining ploy.

Hoarding may occasionally have been the result of the burying of savings for safe-keeping. An example of this is the Otterbourne hoard in which the clipped coins dating from the last years of Roman rule were at the top of the pot. Augustine addressed his audience in North Africa with the apparently familiar image of the owner concealing his hoard in the ground for fear that his or her slave might come along and make off with it. Ritual explanations should not be completely ignored either. However, very often, the burial of treasure objects must have been an emergency act. The case appears obvious that hoarding, or rather non-recovery of hoards, will take place most frequently in troubled circumstances. Bradley analysed the frequency of coin hoards in seventeenth-century England. These amount to one found on average every two years before and after the Civil War, compared with over four per year dating from the period of its duration.

The danger does not have to be attributed to the presence of barbarians. There is a minor wave of hoards, from Gaul and the Rhine, in the years when Constantius II was putting down his rival Magnentius (350-3), but an absence of hoards for the years when Gaul became 'one huge funeral pyre' after 406. If civil war or unrest is one context for deposition and loss, persecution is another, as has been argued concerning the pagan (cult of Faunus) Thetford treasure in the context of the Theodosian edict making sacrifice illegal in 391. The early fifth century presents a complex depositional picture, with nothing much found in Gaul, some hoards on the Rhine, lots of treasures and coins in Britain, some coins only in Spain, and both treasure objects and coins in Italy. A small burst of hoards in the Netherlands and on the Rhine during the second quarter of the fifth century has been attributed to Aetius and the last counterattacks against the Franks, seemingly beyond the imperial borders. Against these examples, the intensity of deposition with the end of the British provinces of the empire is clear: five hoards from this date have been found around Thetford in Norfolk alone, for example. The treasure objects are biased toward the east, whilst coin hoards are biased slightly toward the south-west. But overall East Anglia shows a total weight of precious metals greater than the rest of Britain put together. This figure, however, is distorted by the effects of the huge Hoxne hoard. This was a civilian area yet with a limited tradition of villa construction which may suggest a less entrenched social hierarchy. Maybe social problems general across Britain were worst in this particular area?

An answer to this diversity across Britain and north-west Europe may lie in the difference between sudden social trauma and rumbling uncertainty. There is clear archaeological evidence of a dramatic and comprehensive economic collapse in late fourth- and early fifth-century Britain which is not replicated in suddenness across most of Gaul. The supposed restoration of order in Roman Britain after the barbarian incursions of 367 may not have been long-lived. From the late fourth century, coin clipping, a phenomenon that was kept under strict control in most of the empire, became ever more prevalent in Britain. It has been argued that this clipping occurred in a regulated fashion as a reaction to shortage of coin. However, even if this is true, the clipping is still likely to be a sign of the severe decay of imperial authority and resources in the province of Britain. Some writers have conjured up an image of Britain as being a problem province. We know some interesting facts about the status of Britain in the mid- to later fourth century. In a series of epigrams Ausonius made fun of a Briton called Silvius 'Bonus' (good); for example, 'Silvius is called Good and called a Briton. Who would believe that a good citizen had sunk so low?' Clearly Britons had a poor reputation, and Britain was a place where people could be sent into exile. There was a tendency to rebellion and trouble. When imperial interference took place it is not always clear that this was against *external* troublemakers.

In an early fifth-century Gallic text, Querolus, the eponymous protagonist, asks his household god (*lar familiaris*) how he can have power.

> Querolus: I want to be able to rob those who do not owe me anything and kill the others – I want to be able to rob and kill even my neighbours!
> Lar: You are seeking brigandage not power [legitimate office]. I don't know how to get that for you. Wait! I know. You've just about got what you want. Go and live by the Loire.
> Querolus: What happens there?

Lar: There men live by the law of nations, with no fraud. Capital offences are pronounced under an oak tree and recorded on bones. There rustics give speeches and private citizens pronounce judgement – there everything's allowed!

This picture almost evokes social revolution. The break from Roman law was crucial as this was a key element in Roman identity. The Gallic grandee Rutilius Namatianus celebrated a certain Exuperantius who, in Aremorica (Britanny and the Loire), 're-establishes the laws and freedom and won't let people be their servant's slaves'. And the Gallic Chronicle attests that Brittany 'broke from Roman society', just as Gildas told us that Britain was 'still Roman in name, but not in custom nor in law'.

The first significant mentions of bacaudae (bandits) come in the late third century. Then, a century later, the word (if not exactly the same phenomenon) crops up in the work of the Greek historian Zosimus when Aremorica beyond the Loire was 'in the grip of bacaudic *revolution*' [my italics] (c.407-11). The disadvantaged under the old order may have risen up – an idea pushed by the Marxist historian Thompson. This idea, however, runs into problems over the degree of development of class-consciousness, since, at least in the early Middle Ages, there are few signs of such a phenomenon. The current picture of such events, however, is one of local leadership, in opposition to Thompson's earlier view of social revolution due to a rising of the oppressed poor.

The indigent lower orders were, perhaps, likely to seek the protection of landlords who collected taxes from the peasantry and who were viewed as having rebelled if they withheld funds from the central government. Certainly, we cannot rest with the imperial government's downgrading of serious revolts into mere 'banditry'. Hobsbawm has provided perhaps the major study in recent societies of this phenomenon, which he defines as 'social banditry', that is not just robbery with violence as seen by the state, but 'a form of individual or minority rebellion within peasant societies', a revolt not for a communist utopia, but for a return to old certainties against perceived recent oppression. Lewin modified this to stress that although bandits normally acted from selfish motives and not for the poor of their areas, 'nevertheless, as a vicarious executor of the inarticulate rage of most of the rural poor, the *congaceiro* [Brazilian bandit] had popular appeal.' It is clear from Salvian that the bacaudae were to be found in areas that were under neither barbarian nor Roman [imperial] control. These were people acting in their own interests. They would probably have called themselves Romans, yet may well have resisted re-incorporation into the empire and would certainly not have called themselves bandits.

Whether the rebels were led by aristocrats, or whether the instability extended to social revolution with peasants dispossessing their landlords, the potential for disorder was tremendous in the wake of the collapse of the Roman military system. The revolt in Brittany was such as to lead the Roman general Aetius to send Goar, king of the Alans, with his army into the area, whose advance was only checked by St Germanus of Auxerre. Such a society was potentially far more unstable than one in which a largely barbarian army continued in control, albeit no longer answering to the emperor. In Britain there was a period in the early fifth century of absence of both Roman imperial and royal barbarian control and, thus, the situation mentioned in Querolus may well have been paralleled on a grand scale. Zosimus wrote of this period that the Britons 'revolted from Roman rule and lived by themselves, no longer obeying Roman laws . . . expelling the Roman officials and setting up their own admin-istration as well as they could'.

The emperor Honorius may have issued a command early in the fifth century – may because it is not absolutely clear it relates to Britain – which called on the cities of the island to look to their own defence. This was not intended to condone social revolution or rebellion, but to allow elites legiti-mately to take charge of local military affairs. Honorius encouraged provin-cials to see to the defence of their own property and his relatives in Spain did just that. A further edict broke with centuries of tradition by recommending that even slaves be armed to fight with their owners for their country! If some form of social revolt was a reality in the provinces, this edict would provide good evidence for the disconnection of the imperial court from the realities of the north. According to Gildas, at a date most often interpreted as the mid-fifth century, the 'groans of the Britons' were sent to the Romans as a cry for help. There may have been a pro- and an anti-Roman party in Britain. But the Britons received no reply from the 'Romans', whom Gildas addresses as foreigners to the island. The bringing in of Saxon federates by the British leader 'Vortigern' was ostensibly against the Picts and Scots, but could have been intended to provide an armed retinue against rebellious Britons.

The wave of non-recovery of depositions in southern Britain should be seen not just in the context of the rising danger of barbarian raids, but also in the light of the chronically unstable nature of the former province in the absence of Roman control, or rather of any control. The difference between lowland Britain and Brittany was that the former was a wealthy region likely to contain abundant precious metal, and so has provided hoards, whilst the latter was poor but close to regions that retained a lively literary tradition in the fifth and sixth centuries, and so appears in the historical if not the archaeological record. The deposition of treasures at times of stress can be seen as an act current across late Roman society, but it is the high level of non-recovery that is telling. Waves of unclaimed treasure hoards may indeed demand dramatic contexts, as I suggested with my analogy from present-day Bosnia. The crisis of the Romano-British aristocracy saw the end of the opulent villas and town houses of the fourth century. Romanised values, including those of Christianity, appear to have persevered to a higher degree in many other provinces. The crucial question for the maintenance of some social stability may have been whether there was an individual who could hope to provide order and restitution, whether that person be a Roman judge, a Germanic warlord or a bishop. A power vacuum may have been far more destructive than the replacement, say, of the last western emperor by a barbarian king, and such a vacuum may have been productive of far greater instability leading to the abandonment of treasures.

This view may underestimate the ability of local people in Britain to negotiate amongst themselves, as in the private agreements, *convenientiae*, known from the Continent. However, mediation would have been difficult in the case of conflict between assertion of peasant independence and aristocratic patronage. Although all societies are to some extent predicated upon violence, and violence was endemic in early medieval Francia, systems of law and order existed there. However, it can be argued that in circumstances of rapid change such social controls may not have had time to be established. Any contemporary laws may not have been worth the bones they were scratched on. If there is a great cluster of unclaimed depositions it suggests that whole families were dislocated, since someone would usually know where the household wealth was hidden. The material evidence for the Romano-British aristocracy vanishes in this period. Perhaps the crisis of the aristocracy was greatest in Britain and, if they started the rebellion, it is not at all clear that they ultimately profited from it.

Not only pillage and destruction, but also negotiation and control between the Roman aristocracy and Germanic leaders were important factors in Gaul, but it seems that in Britain the majority of the old elite appears not to have been able to use its wealth to buy survival. The reason is not hard to find: as Esmonde Cleary concludes, 'there was no slow drawing-down of blinds: the end [of Roman Britain] was nasty, brutish and short', and it happened before the substantial arrival of Anglo-Saxons in the mid-fifth century. Ken Dark has mounted a concerted challenge to this view. Arguing from evidence for Latin literacy, he posits the widespread persistence of 'Romanitas'. But this society was clearly very different from the Roman world. It could not have worked in the same way, to take one example, because there was no coinage and no unified standing army. To say that the end of Roman Britain was peaceful means flying in the face of both the literary evidence of Gildas, contemporary texts from the Continent and the overwhelming archaeological evidence for massive economic discontinuity.

In Levi-Strauss' view gift-exchanges, in effect payments, were 'peacefully resolved wars'. In Britain, political breakdown was sudden and the subsequent Germanic takeover was gradual. The allotment system used for the Visigothic settlement in south-west Gaul has been described as 'an imaginative experiment that got a little out of hand'. Nevertheless, the fall or transfer of other regions of the west into organised 'barbarian' hands was often much more rapid and organised than in Britain. This fact may have been the salvation of what remained of the Continental Romanised aristocracy and its culture, rather than its destruction. This is not to say that the old Gallo-Roman elites suffered no losses in wealth and status. It is clear that many aspects of the physical splendour of the Roman elites were vanishing not as a result of barbarian takeover, nor of Christianisation, but due to the unstable political circumstances of the early medieval world.

7 Palaces of God

The collapse of Roman power happened in a sporadic manner across Europe. The eastern heartlands of the empire held out whilst many frontier areas fragmented away. This chapter examines the position of the Church during this age of political turmoil. Whilst the monumental traditions of the State, and of many aristocratic families, collapsed, ostentatious Christianity – in Gaul, if less so in Britain – rose to take its place. Elements of the western nobility, particularly in Rome, struggled unsuccessfully against the rise of Christian power. By the fifth century, however, local elites were generally converted and, at least in Gaul, gained widespread control of appointment to bishoprics, with the result that church-building and Christian artistic patronage became the foci of aristocratic donations to local communities in late antiquity and the early Middle Ages. In classical Roman society, a notable was expected to provide an abundance of gifts to the community as a show of status and patronage. It appears that old ideals of personal fame from public building and giving had resurfaced in a new context. The Church gained prestige in the fourth century because of its adoption of imperial styles of art and symbolism. With the fading of Roman power in the fifth century the magnificence of churches was understood as an image of Paradise. The remote power of the emperor was eclipsed by the greater authority of God, leaving the prestige of the Church and the symbolic power of its buildings enhanced even though its imperial protector was but a shadow of its former self in western Europe.

Christianity, to state the obvious, originated at the far end of the empire from Britain. It is hardly surprising that its rise was slow there during the fourth century. Several pagan temples were refurbished during this period. That at Lydney, for example, was given new mosaic floors. It is not unreasonable to suggest that there is plentiful evidence that British paganism was in excellent health at the end of the century, although it is only fair to note that the temples saw the same collapse in construction as did other classes of site at the end of the Roman period. Failure of the Christianisation of the landscape beyond a few towns, forts or estate centres might suggest weakness of imperial control.

On the other hand, we should perhaps be wary of rushing to read the evidence in terms of either pagan survival or Christian ascendancy. Paganism was not a single, easily identifiable phenomenon, but was composed of a variety of forms of religious expression. It is far from easy to identify religious affiliation from the art of the fourth-century aristocracy. Not only was there a degree of syncretism, but non-Christian forms could persist as motifs, even when their pagan symbolic content has been discarded.

There are several explanations for this phenomenon. Precious artefacts were appreciated for the craftsmanship, quite apart from any religious meaning they might once have imparted. The rise of an allegorical mode of viewing in this period, promoted by the efforts of the Church to impart its message via easily understood symbolism, may have led many ancient images to be re-interpreted, such that a pagan goddess might be held to stand for Christian love in this world. An example of this is the appearance of Venus on the lid of the elaborately decorated silver container known as the 'Projecta casket' after the name of the woman for whom it was made.

The casket is one item in a collection of silverware which was brought to light in 1793 on the slopes of the Esquiline Hill in Rome. This treasure represents a portion of the domestic goods of a wealthy Roman family: clues to which family are provided by inscriptions which mention Turcius Secundus and his wife Projecta, a second female member of the gens Turcia, and a third woman called Pelegrina. The Turcii were a prominent Roman family, members of which attained the offices of governor, *corrector*, suffect consul and consul during the fourth century. The furniture fittings are thought to carry associations of high public office. Dating of the assemblage, on stylistic grounds and with reference to the inscriptions, has been made to the mid-fourth century. On the evidence of wear, the pieces were buried at the turn of the fourth and fifth centuries. The pieces show a variety of Christian and pagan imagery. Perhaps the most important items are the caskets and furniture revetments. The casket of Projecta (l. 54.9 x w. 43.1 x h. 27.9cm) is interpreted as a silver and gilt bridal item. The inscription, SECUNDEET-PROIECTA VIVATIS IN CHRI[STO] ('Secundus and Projecta, may you live in Christ'), identifies the couple, who are further depicted on the lid, whilst elsewhere there are scenes understood as representing bathing, dressing and other rituals appropriate to a traditional Roman marriage.

Such pagan images on objects owned by Christians might then have been understood as secular emblems referring to the good life on this earth. The toilet of Venus would become the visual simile of the toilet of the Roman matron for whom this vanity case was made, functioning not as a reference to pagan cult but as a flattering analogy. Increasingly, the externals, rather than the substance, of traditional modes and images survived either as lingering conventions or as affected signs of high culture. The resulting complexities of the fourth-century material may be illustrated by the mosaic floor at Hinton St Mary that shows both pagan mythology and the head of Christ.

However much polemics sought to establish distance between the different faiths, or even between different versions of the same faith, the fact remains that all were using related visual languages during the fourth century. It is probably not worth the effort to argue over whether certain artistic motifs are 'Jewish' or 'Christian', or indeed 'pagan'. For instance, the motif of a vine

25 & 26 These late antique sarcophagi from Ravenna display the cross, but the images of animals, shells and trees are standard classical symbols of life

25   Late antique sarcophagus, San Vitale, Ravenna

26 Late antique sarcophagus, Archiepiscopal Museum, Ravenna

117

27 & 28   *Defeated barbarians and the fruits of the harvest adorn the funerary monuments*
           to Constantine's family
27   *Sarcophagus of Helena, mother of Constantine, porphyry, Vatican*

28 *Sarcophagus of Constantina, daughter of Constantine, porphyry, Vatican*

growing from a wine cup was employed by and gave the same meaning of 'life' to all three groups. At this date there was simply not a wholly different culture to distinguish Christians from their pagan peers. Christians filled up their lives with images, and even celebrations, derived from the Roman past such that the secularity of large areas of the society of the Christian Roman Empire, therefore, stood massively intact. Christianity can thus be seen to have soaked up much of late antique culture like a sponge. When other institutions of the classical world fell away, the Church was left as the preserver of a cultural legacy which it now cherished as being special to itself.

Churches in post-Roman Gaul

The grand churches of the Mediterranean basin that survive today are not matched by similar examples from the northernmost provinces of the empire. Is this an indication of poverty, or of provincial isolation and conservatism; of pagan influence from beyond the frontiers, or of the strength of native, even perhaps pre-Roman, religious traditions? The question of how strong paganism was in the provincial west is a very thorny one indeed. There are hardly any secure inscriptions for fourth-century religion in Britain, where the overall epigraphic record from the period is very poor. It has been argued, on the evidence of literary high culture in Italy, that there was even a pagan revival across western Europe at the end of the fourth century. Whilst Christianity was most firmly established in the cities of Gaul at the beginning of the fifth century, it was amongst the peasantry that pagan practices may have proved most persistent. Certainly there were Christian denunciations of 'pagan superstition' right through until the sixth century and beyond. It can be suggested that, despite the written evidence of repeated condemnation of 'pagan superstition' by Frankish clerics, paganism was strongly on the decline even in the fourth century, and that the Germanic invasions did not reverse the process, save on the north-eastern fringes of Gaul. On the other hand, Averil Cameron has commented on the same denunciations in Byzantium lasting down to that of a council held in the capital in 692, that 'there is no reason to doubt that competing religious attachments coexisted then just as they do today'. The key to the problem may lie in the definition of paganism. Even if sacrifices to pagan gods had ceased, all manner of other practices, from dancing in the streets on the Kalends of January to the making of medical potions from herbs, could be derided as being 'pagan' in so far as their ritual efficacy was not dependent on the Church and the liturgy.

Sulpicius Severus' biography of Martin, bishop of Tours in north-western France, was one of the great 'bestseller' texts of the period. Bishop from 371-90, he gave battle against 'pagani', that is 'rustics', who were clinging to the old customs. Stancliffe finds Martin's campaign against paganism plausible, with Severus' account being misleading only in not revealing what other

Christian leaders were very likely doing along the same lines. Further indications of the spread of Christianity into the countryside of northern Gaul come from Victricius of Rouen. It is, however, a little startling to juxtapose the words of Remigius of Rheims to Clovis in 481 or 486, 'great news has reached us, that you have taken up the government of Belgica Secunda. It is no new thing that you would begin to be what your parents were', with the fact that Clovis did not convert to Catholic Christianity for some time afterward (although he may have had an intervening Arian heretical period). It is a testament to the crumbling of late Roman cultural authority that the government of this area of northern Gaul was in pagan hands at the end of the fifth century. The same may be said of eastern Britain, where Christianity was not to regain the upper hand for over a century.

Towns were the centres of religious authority. Indeed a number of bishops from British towns attended church councils in the fourth century, from London and York particularly, but we have a poor level of evidence for basilican churches from towns in Britain, which provides a sharp contrast to many areas of the Continent, where there was a lively tradition of church-building, and where churches were the one major category of monumental building in the early Middle Ages. The presence of a bishop can be seen as an important factor in the survival of a town in early medieval Gaul. The cities there seem to have had suburban basilicas, along with the cathedral, as their main foci.

The aristocratic and Christian domination of towns in late sixth-century Gaul emerges powerfully in the texts written by Gregory, bishop of Tours, a noble whose life and career had been permeated and shaped by relations with his patron saints. The audience of Gregory's histories, both ecclesiastical and lay, was composed of people of high status. The 'humble style' used by Gregory can be seen as a result of the prestige of Biblical low style in Christian polemic. We can interpret his *Histories* as satirising other sources of power, particularly those of the Frankish courts, as part of the defence strategy of a Roman aristocracy that constituted a large proportion of the upper ranks of the Church in late antique Gaul.

Individual noble families virtually monopolised episcopal office-holding in certain towns. Royal control was limited to attempts to assert the right of confirmation of elections, to the holding of synods, and to desperate measures such as the abduction of bishop Theodore of Marseille and the murder of bishop Praetextatus of Rouen. A picture of intense local power and control can be reconstructed for sixth-century bishops in Gaul. They possessed both economic and spiritual prestige and were important in the maintenance of urban centres. The only local official who could challenge their authority was the *comes civitatis* (count of the city), who himself could be deposed, as the machinations against Leudast of Tours show.

Many of these bishops were intent on building churches that were decorated in the grand late antique style, with gold and silver treasures, wall paintings, marbles and mosaics. Exempla were provided by the surviving buildings of the fourth century. Gold mosaic cubes have been found from the great late Roman double cathedral at Trier showing that the luxurious style of Italian basilicas was replicated in the north. Furthermore, Gregory of Tours tells of a church in Cologne dedicated to the martyrs of the Theban Roman Legion, but 'because the church, with its wonderful construction and mosaics, shines as if somehow gilded, the inhabitants like to call it the "church of the golden saints"'. Although surviving examples are very rare, the mosaic expert Barral I Altet asserts, based on the literary evidence, that 'it cannot be doubted that the techniques of mosaic have been used without interruption to decorate the walls of the churches of Gaul from the fifth to the ninth centuries, as they had been in the Christian east and in Italy'.

Sidonius, bishop of Clermont, wrote of a new fifth-century church at Lyons that 'the sun is drawn to the gilded ceiling as it passes over the warm-hued metal, matching its colour. Marble in different shades gleams across the vaults, floor and windows: and below the multicoloured windows a green lawn of sapphire stones is tinged with emerald glass.' As Ian Wood has argued, there was lively competition in church building in early medieval Gaul and 'for a period of supposed urban decline, the amount of ecclesiastical building and the overriding image of the holy city can seem curiously out of place'. Namatius of Clermont-Ferrand built a church in the mid-fifth century in the city with walls round the sanctuary of 'mosaic work made of many varieties of marble'. And we are told of Agricola, bishop of Chalons who died *c.*580, that 'he came from a senatorial family and was known for his wisdom and refinement. He erected many buildings in the city, put up houses and built the cathedral which was supported by columns, adorned with marble and decorated with mosaics.'

The art of these churches must be held to encompass the movables as well as the fixtures of these buildings. Fifth- to seventh-century Gallic wills show us the considerable quantities of treasure given to churches, as in the extraordinary list of plate given by Desiderius of Auxerre to two churches which at 137kg adds up to over six times the weight of one of the greatest late antique British treasures, that found at Mildenhall. Peter Brown has emphasised the fact that churches were attempts to provide an experience of heaven on earth. The otherworld was a precise place, he writes: 'the solemn liturgy, the blaze of lights, the shimmering mosaics, and the brightly coloured curtains of a late antique church were there to be appreciated in their entirety . . . Taken together, they provide a glimpse of paradise.' These churches, with their abundance of precious liturgical plate, were an obvious target for looters. But they were protected, as villas and other secular buildings were not, by their sacral nature.

We have seen that there were varied local responses to instability. Aristocrats in Gaul placed increasing reliance upon personal defences, both physical, as in Nicetius of Trier's castle, with its towers and catapult, and also ideological: Nicetius was the bishop and he seems to have placed relics there. During this period the landed aristocracy in Gaul focused on the episcopacy as its central institution. This represents a major change from the fourth to the fifth centuries as the aristocracy altered its models of prestige and the Church was less frequently staffed by individuals of lower rank. *Romanitas* had meant adherence to an elite cultural tradition and the preservation of the traditional privileges of the elite. The Church provided the possibility, under the patronage of God and the saints, of retaining prestige and gaining personal protection.

Churches in post-Roman Britain

There were two phases of Christianisation in Britain: the first during the fourth and fifth centuries, which was considerably disrupted by the invasion of the pagan Anglo-Saxons, and the second which saw the reintroduction of Christianity to lowland England in the seventh century via both Roman and Celtic missions. In much of Roman Britain it seems that there had been a failure of Christianity to spread widely. This can be seen in terms of the strong persistence of Celtic paganism and general weakness of 'Romanisation'. Romano-Celtic temples were not an insular phenomenon. In all their forms, square, round and polygonal, they are found in southern Britain and Gaul, with a few on the Danube, although not in northern Britain and Ireland. The peak in the numbers of such temples comes in the second century on the Continent, but in the fourth century in Britain, although urban temples decline from the beginning of that century. There are 14 temples listed by Painter where numbers of very late coins are large enough to suggest votives rather than losses, the greatest example being Lydney with over 6000. The pagan Thetford treasure would seem to show some sort of reasonably wealthy support, even if this was buried at a time of persecution. In the south-west of sub-Roman Britain we can find perhaps a dozen or so sites with survival, if not proof of cult, into the fifth century, together with the creation of some new sites. At Maiden Castle a temple was built in the late fourth century, whilst at Frilford there was building work and coins from *c*.350-400.

Britain in the early fourth century was in the mainstream of contemporary Roman art and was perhaps at its wealthiest as a province. Yet it is hard to conclude that the Church was anything other than poor and rather underdeveloped. The maximal view was given in the earlier work of Dorothy Watts who then wished to identify as many objects as possible as indicating the one-time presence of Christian belief, producing a 'density map' of Christianity in the later fourth century. Yet a different survey of small finds found only 70 out of a total of 260 which had 'definite Christian significance'. The most likely places to produce such items were not towns, as we might expect from Continental parallels, but forts and villas. Watts identified a number of 'almost certain' Romano-British churches, including Butt Rd, Colchester; St Paul in the Bail, Lincoln; Richborough; St Pancras, Canterbury; Silchester;

Icklingham; Uley Buildings 7 and 8; and Witham, with other house chapels at Chedworth, Frampton, Hinton St Mary, Littlecote, Lullingstone, St Mary de Lode and Woodchester.

The attribution of most of these sites is debatable. For example at Uley, phase 6 shows a partial collapse of the old temple in the late fourth century, together with a find of a folded plaque with Biblical scenes. This, it must be stressed, does not prove Christian worship at the site. And nor does phase 7a, timber buildings, including one looking like a hall. However, in phase 7b, a small chapel was built at some point during the early Middle Ages. Uley has post-Roman window glass with parallels at Jarrow, Monkwearmouth and Whitby, suggesting a seventh- rather than a fourth- or fifth-century date. A potentially more important example is the major late Roman building cut into deposits of *c*.350 at the eastern side of London. This may turn out to have been the city's cathedral, since it shares similarities in plan with Continental Christian basilicas. An apsed building has recently been found at Vindolanda which is similar to a structure at Housteads. There is no proof, at present, that this is a church, although it is definitely post-400 and unlikely to be Anglo-Saxon.

Many of these sites are only identified because of their ground plan, which is hardly a safe basis for an attribution. Amongst the more likely candidates, the Richborough building shows lines of blocks which carried a timber superstructure, not securely dated, but a foot higher than coins of *c*.340, suggesting a date from the end of the fourth century to the early fifth. This shore fort was one of the last sites to be manned by the State (in the form of soldiers paid by Constantine III). If Christianity was heavily dependent upon state patronage, it is easy to understand forts as centres of the religion, whilst, if aristocratic patronage of towns had collapsed, it is easy to understand the weakness of evidence from urban centres. To give one example of this, the presumed Silchester 'church' provides one of the best examples of its kind from Britain, but there is still no definite proof of its identity, and 50 people would have had trouble squeezing in. The apse, which has been used as one piece of evidence for this building's attribution, was a feature only expected from the sixth century onward in churches. It has even been suggested that the building may have been the temple of an eastern cult. Occupation ended in 'squatter' use, *c*.370. The Lincoln church, like many others of which nothing much has survived, was wooden. Only very occasionally does a more recognisably Christian topography emerge, as at Icklingham with its baptismal font, east–west graves and building 'B' which was identified as a church. This site is, however, a conspicuous exception.

Why this lack of architectural evidence? A major factor is the dramatic collapse of the Roman province which saw towns and villas suddenly abandoned. There was no such disastrous crash in most of Gaul. In Italy many of the late antique churches have continually been places for worship and their Roman decorations have been preserved for us. We have to go

29 *Head of Christ, mosaic, fourth century AD, Hinton St Mary, Dorset.*
Copyright British Museum.

on archaeological plans for Britain since there is a lack of standing walls, or
we must rely on finding objects with Christian symbols such as the Chi
Rho or Alpha Omega, or specifically Christian scenes. However, as has
already been noted, the presence of a motif does not necessarily prove the
presence of a belief.

We do have more clearly Christian art works, for example the mosaic at
the villa of Hinton St Mary with its head of Christ, or Lullingstone villa's
praying figures done in painted plaster which are now on show at the British
Museum. These may indicate villa chapels (Gallic villas could be praised for
the prominence of their chapels). Some artefacts are also pretty much unambiguous in their affiliation. The Water Newton silver treasure consists of two
goblets, a dish and a wine strainer with Christian symbols. This was clearly a
communion set. Another important artefact is the Risley Park lanx which has
Christian symbols and bears the name of a certain Bishop Exuperius. Burials
have also been seen as a convenient way of distinguishing pagan from
Christian populations, but this is not so – we cannot say much about religious
affiliation from the provision or otherwise of grave goods.

However much Christianity had grown in fourth-century Britain, its spread is obscured for us by the decline in construction and production in the province. In contrast, Christianity appears to have steadily become prominent in post-Roman Britain after the end of imperial administration *c.*410, if the evidence of the life of St Germanus can be trusted. Pelagianism, the heresy that occasioned his visit, had been started by a Briton. During Germanus' visit to Britain, victory was achieved against a group of invaders by shouting 'hallelujah!' at the crucial point in a battle. The theme of military triumph through faith is interesting, since this may have been the key to the spread of Christianity in those troubled times. Germanus is also described as having been met by well-dressed citizens at St Albans, where Bede said miracles had not ceased from the time of the martyrdom in the third century to his own day. The sixth-century *Passio Albani* has Germanus visit the shrine. This all sounds like good evidence for widespread Christianity, but we may note that St Albans does show signs of late urban life, and was perhaps atypical. Also we might note that Germanus had to hold a mass baptism of the British troops before the 'hallelujah victory' in 429, even if their leaders were already Christian.

The evidence of Patrick, Gildas and contemporary inscriptions testify to the ultimate victory of Christianity in the early medieval west of Britain. It is a matter of conjecture where St Patrick was born. Native Irish sources suggest the late fifth century for Patrick's death date. However, in 431 Pope Celestine had appointed Palladius bishop of the Irish. Patrick was, therefore, not the first bishop of Ireland and Augustine's not the first mission to the British Isles from Rome. For decades there was, in all probability, a dispersion of Christian slaves and soldiers beyond the frontiers. We should think in terms of varied communities of the faithful, since there was no single 'Celtic Church'. By the time of the rise of the early medieval textual tradition, monasticism was crucially important, although in the sense of being highly organised with a Rule, there is little clear evidence before the sixth century.

By the later fifth century British kings had adopted Christianity, but their power was increasingly limited by the Anglo-Saxon monarchies. The immigration of the pagan Anglo-Saxons may have been the spur to the Christianisation of those Britons who did not assimilate with the newcomers but who succeeded in asserting their difference and independence in opposition to the foreigners. Celtic was apparently still the majority language at the end of the Roman period. It might appear that the English were so unimpressed by what they found that they ignored both insular language and religion. This intransigence contrasts with the rapid conversion of much of England in the seventh century (with Celtic assistance), which has been seen as a testimony to the then power of the Anglo-Saxon rulers, perhaps linked to the quasi-religious role of early Germanic kings as links between their people and the gods.

Seen in the general perspective of European culture, Britain seems to have experienced an arrested development of Christianity. There are two main hypotheses concerning this problem. One assumes that there was rapid Christianisation in all areas of the empire while under Roman rule. The lack of evidence from Britain is, therefore, considered to be because of trends in building and manufacture. Early medieval Wales was strongly Christianised but has left precious few traces of substantial church buildings because either these were not built, or have not survived because most construction was executed in wood. Christianity continued to exist in those areas which had not been taken over by the Anglo-Saxons through the early Middle Ages, resulting in the remaining church of the Celts which debated the correct date of Easter with the representatives of the newly established Church in seventh-century England.

That is one possibility. The other is that there are few traces of Christianity in later Roman Britain because there *was* little Christianity in later Roman Britain. This view emphasises that Britain was at the limit of the Roman world and was far away from the main cultural centres of the empire. Whereas Africa had had substantial Christian communities even in the third century, the religion was late to arrive in Britain. A recent survey of Christian date of death inscriptions produced some fascinating results. The tabulated figures show the percentage of inscriptions per year from 310 to 710, rather than the absolute number of inscriptions. So there must be some room for error bearing in mind wide variations in the number of inscriptions from region to region over time. However, the broad trend does appear clearly. North Africa peaks from 360 to 460, whilst Italy is the only other region rising sharply during the last period of the empire in the west. All other Continental regions, including Gaul, then peak around 560.

Inscribing Christian forms in date of death inscriptions was in vogue first in Africa, then Italy, before spreading widely across Spain and Gaul, a process which only takes off there around 460 and reaches its height a century later. In Britain, with the towns impoverished, the aristocracy conservative and the presence of imperial officials and troops small and diminishing, there was little to spread Christian fervour before the collapse of imperial law. But to put Britain in context it has been remarked by Thébert that 'the extreme scarcity of overtly Christian motifs in the late mosaics of wealthy African homes is striking. One has to wonder whether Christianity penetrated the African ruling class until quite late, the fifth century at the earliest'!

The evidence is not easy to interpret yet it is likely that the British church was small and poor and that few towns had bishops; it is probable too that although Christianity was gaining ground through the fourth century, its progress is obscure to us due to the inadequacies of our source evidence. The Christianity that was to characterise the Celtic church was not monumental in scale and so it is hard to pick out from the traces of everyday life. Roman society was strongly monumental in its architecture, imagery and ritual, which is why it is much easier for us to identify classical symbolism: the Roman way was to write achievements in masonry, boldly and to last. Christianity did triumph in the post-Roman west of Britain. It has been argued that it was the very weakness of the elite that allowed this. Christianity offered a new way of holding communities together, especially once they were fighting pagan Germanic enemies, and the social destabilisation of the old Roman elite may have had an important part to play in this process. In Gaul the aristocracy increasingly used the Church as a vehicle for their classical cultural values from the fifth century. In Britain, Roman control ceased before the Church had become a focus for the landed elite and the one could not buttress the other and share in its culture to anything like the same degree as in much of Gaul.

Villas and monasteries

An important element of the transition from Roman to medieval life on the Continent was that many villas may have become the bases for monasteries in the post-Roman period, with continuance of worship in their house chapels. Sidonius Apollinaris found a friend of his much changed, living frugally as a monk in his villa which was sparsely furnished with stools, hard couches and hangings of horsehair. Sulpicius Severus at Primuliacrum and Paulinus at Nola set up religious communities around themselves and their dwelling-places at the turn of the fourth and fifth centuries. We should think perhaps of a continuum extending from the traditional Roman aristocratic pursuit of *otium*. Archaeological excavation on the monastic sites of Ligugé near Poitiers, and at Marmoutier, has shown the reuse and redevelopment of Roman buildings, such that we should not assume that conversion to monastic use was simply a passive process in architectural terms.

Sorde-l'Abbeye, near Dax in south-west Gaul, may show us what forms continuity of use could take. A Roman building with splendid mosaics provides the footings for many of the walls of a later monastery. There is no evidence of destruction, but rather of building to link the original residential and bath blocks by the construction of a colonnade at a late, perhaps sixth-century, date. There are nine mosaic pavements, half in the residential block, dated on stylistic parallels from North Africa, some to the fifth, and others to the sixth or even early seventh centuries. The move toward spending on public areas of the house is mirrored at other sites with late mosaics, such as St Sever, Labastide and Séviac. The last of these sites shows evolution rather then degradation in the fifth century, including the installation at the end of that century of what has been identified as a baptismal pool with a church nearby.

Parallels to any of this in Britain are hard to spot since the material culture of the Britons appears to have been so impoverished. We are left with speculation, such as the suggestion that Lullingstone may have been developing as a monastic site. A possible example has, however, been identified on the site of the early fifth-century cemetery next to Poundbury hillfort outside Dorchester. The late Roman sequence include clusters of stone mausolea which appear to have been integrated, perhaps as churches, into a post-Roman sequence of buildings using drystone and wood. This arrangement may represent an interesting post-Roman development since one may contrast the uniform graves of the late Roman period with the increasing clustering, focal graves, cairns and ditches to be found in the early medieval Celtic west, as for example at Plas Gogerddan in Wales. Similar types and techniques to those in use at Poundbury appear in the post-Roman structures erected in Wroxeter, save with timber superstructures resting on rubble platforms.

The crucial problem with these sites is the lack of datable artefacts. The buildings were attributed primarily using carbon-14 dating and through the relationship of sequences to the late Roman material. The overall picture of the end of late Roman rural occupation in Britain is not so much of construction or destruction as slow recession and decay, with so-called 'squatter' occupation as a last stage. Most sites, including the postulated monastic settlement at Poundbury, failed to make the transition into the later medieval centuries, perhaps due to an intervening pagan period with English settlement.

This is not to say that everything in comparison is straightforward in Gaul. There are major problems in identifying, for example, an early medieval building with Roman walls for its foundations, or a villa put into service as a monastery, or an urban house used by monks. Masonry was not used exclusively. From the early medieval period, perhaps one of the better descriptions that we have of a rural monastery was that at Condat which was built of wood. We also need to rethink our sense of what represents reuse or decay. There are many Gallic sites with burials in villas that cut through mosaic floors. These may look like degenerate acts, but why go to the trouble of digging through floorings? Maybe such pavements were symbolically associated with Christian burial in the early Middle Ages?

Saints as patrons

In much of Gaul the Church flourished during the late Roman as opposed to only in the post-Roman period. It prevailed, along with major elements of the old landed elites, in an alliance of mutual patronage and support. Lands and property were vulnerable, but God watched over his own. Gregory of Tours tells us how this happened by explaining what took place in the thriving city of Bordeaux, where bishop Severinus was buried. Because his holiness was recognised, 'the local inhabitants thereafter took him as their patron. They knew that whenever their city was either invaded by an illness or besieged by some enemy or disrupted by some vendetta, they would immediately be delivered from this threatening disaster as soon as the people gathered at the church of the saint, observed fasts, celebrated vigils and piously offered prayers.' Saints were patrons of their cities, and their bodies in the extramural churches offered a ring of spiritual protection superior to the physical protection offered by the city walls: as Avitus of Vienne wrote 'the city is protected more by its basilicas then by its bastions'. They replicated the empire in spirit, since the saints were courtiers who would petition the God-Emperor for justice and retribution.

Admittedly disaster was not always prevented, as when, as Gregory of Tours noted, 'many churches were plundered by the soldiers of [the early Frankish ruler] Clovis, for he still clung to his pagan idolatries'. But even when the saint did not prevent the atrocity revenge would be visited on the malefactors, as on the occasion, recounted by Gregory, when the Frankish king Guntram had sent an army against Gundovald the pretender whose troops were holed up in Comminges. The attackers came to the church of Vincent at Agen inside which the locals had barricaded themselves with their treasures. Their hope was that 'the shrine of so great a martyr would not be violated by men calling themselves Christians'. The soldiers, however, burnt down the church doors, slaughtered the people and seized both their property and the church plate as well. Yet the saint avenged the desecration: 'the hands of many caught fire supernaturally . . . some were possessed by a devil and rushed about screaming the martyr's name. Others fought with each other and wounded themselves with their own javelins.' Gregory saw some of them later at Tours and could testify that 'they suffered to the end of their present lives from the torture of excruciating pains'.

There are many other examples of such holy vengeance. For instance, a noble claimed a church estate in Aix and obtained a judgement in his favour from the royal court. The bishop closed the local church of St Mitrias, declaring that no more prayers would be said there unless the saint ensured the restitution of the property. The nobleman then fell into a terminal sickness and offered up the land. A certain man who stole some church glass was struck with leprosy, whilst another who took a gold belt left on an altar died of a fractured skull. Yet other thieves were killed in brawls or blinded, whilst one man slipped when attempting to dislodge a gold ornament, stabbed himself in the side and crushed his testicles. Their examples and Gregory's testimony must have acted to warn off many potential attackers.

The presence of patrons and protectors, which had been vital for the operation of Roman society, would have played a key role in the defence of property by providing the threat of punishment for attacks and so reducing their incidence. The Church may not have had its own armies, but it did have the power of the saints, which provided crucial patronage and protection for grand edifices that were otherwise prime targets for looting. Lay aristocrats could raise retinues, but would have to pay heavily for the privilege, thus leaving far less ready cash available for buildings and their decoration. The Church depended on the existing order and achieved a compromise which legitimised private wealth in return for acts of charity. The building and decoration of churches replaced the endowment of temples, and these buildings became the premier repositories of late Roman art and architectural tradition in the Continental early medieval west. The prestige of Roman elite art was now associated with the Church. The persistence of much of such art and architecture was, therefore, strongly bound up with the circumstances in which Christianity established prominence. In Britain this occurred largely in a post-Roman environment and thus the British Church did not have the same architectural inheritance from the Roman world since this had already been lost in society at large. Nor had the British elite taken up control of the Church and so they could not use it to buttress their position at a time when the old contract with the empire had been burnt by the Picts, Scots and Saxons. The architectural simplicity of the Celtic Church derives from this pattern of events, rather than representing a thoroughgoing rejection of ostentation.

Those who pray and those who kill

At Saint-Martin-de-Mondeville, south-east of Caen, the stone constructions of the Roman period went out of use around 300 to be replaced by more rudimentary wooden buildings consisting of a single sunken chamber with a thatched roof supported by posts at the ends. There was little change until the eighth century when there were rising numbers of small finds and some stone buildings. Until recently this pattern would have been understood as the replacement of the Gallic population by Germanic settlers. However, the situation is now regarded as being more complex. There has been a rise in problematising such Sunken Featured Buildings, to suggest that they are a sign of cultural mixing rather than of specifically Germanic settlement. Current French archaeological opinion suggests that SFBs' considerable diffusion during the fourth century could reflect the development of a settlement form common to the whole of north-west Europe without it necessarily being a mark of Germanic expansion.

On the other hand, the increasing prominence of wooden construction in the post-Roman period is still frequently associated with the presence of barbarians. Masonry architecture is often seen as characteristic of the Roman period in north-west Europe, yet building traditions do not always neatly agree with imperial decline and fall. Small-scale secular masonry construction can be found in southern Gaul in the fifth and sixth centuries, but only from the eighth century in the north. Nevertheless, one of the most significant features of the post-Roman world in general was *secular* abandonment of the more ostentatious Roman building styles. This is in distinct contrast to church buildings which, to take the example of northern Gaul, are marked by a wish to recall the architectural and artistic traditions of antiquity. Wood was more often available in the vicinity, it is true, but in Cirencester, for instance, there was plentiful old Roman stone and indeed quarry faces nearby, but almost no stone building other than churches between 425 and 1100. Was this situation something to do with organising labour? If so what about the fact that huge earth dykes were constructed in the early Middle Ages? Or are we, perhaps, seeing a phenomeon that is partly a result of changes in attitudes and fashions as well as shifts in economic realities?

Prestige and power in post-Roman secular society were increasingly identified with adherence to the norms of local kings who differed greatly in their use or appreciation of *Romanitas*. In the post-Roman north-west of Europe the secular elite mostly lived in wooden structures. It is not good enough simply to put this down to 'barbarism' or poverty, since grand churches in the late antique style continued to be constructed on the Continent if not in Britain. We must look for the answer in terms of the spending choices of the aristocracy.

This is partly a question of aesthetics. Praise of marble- and mosaic-clad structures is frequent in late antiquity. It is, therefore, striking to find these techniques called to yield to the craftsmanship of a carpenter, 'for rightly I prefer the woodcarver's artifice', but in a poem written by the Latin poet Venantius Fortunatus this is what happens. Venantius is generally understood as representing late antique Italian traditions transported into the world of early medieval Francia (the Germanic kingdom set up in what had been Roman Gaul). That the poet had an audience in the north is testament to the continued prestige there of certain Roman cultural forms. How was it, then, that he could write seemingly so against the tastes of the ancient aristocracy for whom wooden buildings were inappropriate for stylish living?

Perhaps Venantius can be seen as an important cultural link. Klaus Randsborg has highlighted the potential of studying the period from 300 to 600 as a subject within the greater unity of the first millennium. This model seems particularly attractive in areas such as the western Mediterranean basin where there *was* very considerable continuity of culture from the fourth to the sixth centuries. However, the story in northern Gaul and Britain is rather different. In these areas archaeology shows us the sudden breakdown of the Roman economic system, as large-scale coin use and pottery production declined or even ceased. Yet aristocratic society continued in some form. How did the ideologies of the local landed elites change during this process? It is likely that in a situation of diminishing resources the available cash would have been better spent on buying military support than in ostentatious private building. The undermining of Roman law may have caused instability in landholding, leading to capital dispersion rather than concentration. Or cash, when available, may have been converted into votives for safe-keeping.

In areas where there was greatest continuity of Roman government structures under the new Germanic monarchies the law would replace the need for private action and the old life could continue to a greater extent. But it seems that everywhere the same pressures towards militarisation of the landed elites were being felt. Military elites placed much less emphasis on decorative domestic architecture. Venantius' poem would, therefore, be the product of the changing values of a society in which an old cultural form (Latin poetry) was used to legitimate a new one (wooden building as prestigious dwelling place). Militarisation was not brought in by complete outsiders. The Goths, for example, were settled as agents of the Roman government in south-west Gaul. And it is now perfectly clear that the disappearance of much of Roman material culture in Britain, including the demise of the villas, took place before the establishment of the Anglo-Saxons. In other words, something had happened *within* late Roman culture itself.

As we have seen, entering the Church was one option for civilian survival and fortifying villas was another. A recent archaeological study by Van Ossel has commented on the scarcity of obviously fortified villas in north-east Gaul, apart from the occasional site found in texts such as the Burgus Pontus Leontius which may have been used in emergencies. Unfortunately, fortification is rather hard to see in the material record. How would this show? What if outside walls simply lacked low windows? We may note the conjectural reconstruction of the late villa at Pfalzel, with one main entrance, no windows at ground level and three storeys. How far might we trace such developments in Britain before the collapse of the material record there? Because we only have ground plans, we must rely on evidence such as thickening of lower walls in order to deduce the original presence of upper storeys and, thus, both these and the functions of such architecture are often hard to identify. Thus we do not need to look for a bank or wall around the villa. There are some dramatic late Roman villas in Britain, for example Keynsham in Somerset, where the plans do seem to suggest the presence of corner towers, indicating the prestige of height and of elevations that were, or suggested, fortifications.

Nevertheless, it is interesting to note that a comparative search through Gregory of Tours' references to dwellings suggests that house-fortification was still the exception in early medieval Gaul: as argued by Ross Samson, security for landowners was primarily assured by royal law, rather than by resort to fortifications. In times of danger people did not shut themselves up in their own homes, but went into towns or hilltop refuges, or hid in churches where those seeking sanctuary were defended by the power of the local saint. Recourse to patrons, to the king's court, or to the court of heaven seem to have been the main strategies in the protection of property.

Yet Gallic literary references to villas in general are rarely reflected in the material record. A number of explanations have been offered for this. For example, it has been suggested that many villas became patronal centres for peasants in unstable times. These sites perhaps resembled small villages and have often become invisible under succeeding modern settlements. A second possibility is to focus on the replacement of masonry construction with timber. Literary evidence, if not archaeological survival, provides a mass of documentary evidence for wooden buildings on the Continent. This is not such a revolution as it at first appears, since it is almost certain that the vast majority of buildings in Roman Britain were made of timber and the situation is likely to have been similar in many parts of Gaul. Many British Roman-period structures that appear to have been of stone may only have had stone footings to inhibit rot, and very few indeed were made of stone in the first century. Using solid stone blocks was enormously time-consuming and the usual practice in Britain was to mortar brick or stone facings and then pour in a rubble core, lines of tiles being employed to make up for irregularity in the facing. In these circumstances, we only have to account for the eclipse of a particularly expensive element in construction techniques.

The fact is, of course, that we know extremely little about post-Roman elite dwellings, and this is in sharp contrast to the situation in the imperial centuries. One approach is to stress differences in regional histories. There was no strict uniformity of cultural life under the empire, but rather a set of variations on a theme. In some areas of northern Gaul Van Ossel has identified the major break in art and architecture coming in the third century, rather than later on. Whilst the Burgundian and Gothic governments of southern Gaul maintained a degree of order which allowed traditional models of prestige to be partly retained, we may imagine that with the collapse of the imperial administration in the north that there was something of a power vacuum in Britain and northern Gaul. Moreover, Christianity was weak in these areas, leaving them without a strong network of bishops who could intercede to protect property.

In these circumstances it is hardly surprising if social upheavals were rife, or that spare cash had to be employed in payments to personal retinues of bodyguards. Many estates would have been broken up or could not be reached by bailiffs. There was no longer so much money to spend on luxurious dwellings. There would, further, now be less social competition in terms of domestic accommodation. Prestige appeared in such contexts as personal dress and the size of one's following. Houses were in far greater danger than before of destruction, and society was more mobile, promoting the construction of simpler, cheaper structures of wood. Such dwellings have rarely been preserved in the archaeological record, thus exaggerating the degree of social discontinuity. Stone continued in use for many churches, at least in Gaul, since these were a separate class of buildings the security of which was promoted by relics where these were present. Venantius testifies to a few cases where a bishop renovated ancient masonry villas in south-west Gaul to their former splendour, but, in contrast to continuity in church construction, such domestic tastes appear to have been on the wane even in that region. The Goths had initially supported the old infrastructure, but this situation was far from frozen. Cultural changes were happening slowly there that paralleled those that had already taken place further north. The prestige of certain aspects of Roman culture outlasted the empire in some areas and in some minds, but it had no innate desirability and its degree of persistence is perhaps more remarkable than its decay.

With the early medieval re-establishment of Christianity in eastern Britain, why did the churches end up as the main buildings of stone, with almost everything else in wood? The answer would appear to be that there was a preference for building churches in stone by the priests of the Roman mission since they were used to them, and so as to differentiate the resulting buildings from wooden pagan temples. Wooden buildings for Anglo-Saxon lords were clearly seen as sufficient. The descriptions in the poem *Beowulf*, taken together with the halls at sites such as Yeavering and Cheddar, are quite enough to show us that the prestige of the built environment was significant in English lay society. But the Anglo-Saxons were not concerned to build their halls in the classical style.

The prominence of stone and brick building in the imperial period appears to have been associated with Roman cultural prestige. The degradation of that tradition might be seen in the light not so much of reduced but of more fluid circumstances. If property holding itself were much more unstable there was far less incentive to plunge money into building works. If the villas had been major repositories of treasure goods then they would be an easy and obvious target for looting. We could understand that where there was sufficient stability these ancient villas might have been preserved as relic-protected monasteries. Areas such as Britain, which did not enjoy a Roman-negotiated Germanic settlement, appear to have been considerably more chaotic than those that did, like Gothic south-west Gaul. In Britain the pattern of continuity from villa to monastic church was especially unlikely since Christianity seems to have failed to bloom there in the period before the collapse of Roman material culture in the early fifth century and only re-emerged subsequently. Post-Roman Britons may have continued, at least for a while, to think of themselves as Romans, but their culture, simply through its singular physical invisibility, was not classical.

Even in Gaul the glamour of classicism was to fade in the early Middle Ages as Rome's association with power withered, at least outside the Church with its emphasis on Latin learning. The Continental Church continued to patronise many of the ancient material arts, such as stone building and carving, window-glass manufacture and mosaic, even though these art forms had largely fallen out of use amongst the secular aristocracy. The Church gained prestige from these forms of display and yet, unlike laymen, was helped to protect such investments by the retributive power of the saints, without having to transfer spending from building to military retinues. The secular aristocracy, by contrast, was increasingly dependent on the favour of the Germanic monarchies for land and prestige. In due course the mobile military form of life came to dominate the lay elites, which then acted as patrons of the Church which was the inheritor of much of the intellectual and material culture of the ancient world.

The reintroduction of Roman-style churches from the Continent to Anglo-Saxon England did not lead to a rapid spread of stone architecture into the world of the secular aristocracy. When these forms were reintroduced in the north the meaning of this material culture was Christian rather than imperial. Roman-derived architecture and decoration now pertained to the Church and, therefore, may even have seemed inappropriate in a private context. North-western early medieval society was, in general, characterised by a division between secular and sacred building traditions which had not been present in late antique society. Kings, with the failing of the old Roman tax system, were poorer than Roman governors, as were aristocrats since they were in a situation of less stable property-holding. There was thus less competition and building could take place on a lesser scale and still seem impressive. In association with this reduced scale, there would have been fewer craftsmen, so restricting further building work. Moreover, the collapse of the Roman distributive system would have restricted the supply of materials. It was thus easier to make a big impression using less money. We do not need to postulate the extinction of the ancient elite in order to explain the vanishing of much ancient architectural ostentation. I do not, of course, wish to claim that economic decline and social replacement had no part to play in the widespread abandonment of the grand villas and palaces in north-western Europe, but simply to point out that the fate of secular building in the old style can also be seen in the light of changing cultural self-identities and priorities. In the immediate aftermath of empire, architectural ostentation in the grand Roman manner was, in these remote realms far from the surviving emperors in Byzantium, left in the hands of the Church.

Overview

We have seen that when the Roman empire expanded across the north and west of Europe, elites in those areas were no longer allowed to reward their followers and establish their prestige through traditional military means. Their privileged position was now to be guaranteed by the imperial government. They were to collect rents on their lands and to organise the passing on of taxes to the state. The premier model for power and prestige in their society no longer followed their own tradition but that of the Roman state. This does not mean that these people automatically wanted to be, or thought of themselves as, Roman. The adoption of Roman culture by the elite was an act of self-empowerment. The operation of this may be expressed as 'respect me for what I resemble'. Subordinates knew that the aristocrat no longer had an armed retinue, but still must not be attacked because he would be defended by the Roman army and legal process. A parallel is with the marketing of an unknown author who may be given book jackets that look like those of a well-known and admired competitor. At the same time Romanised display acted as a focus for competition between aristocrats.

Initially, the focus of display was on monumental architecture in towns, but as urban centres came increasingly under the direct control of the imperial government they became more effective symbols of the prestige of the State than of local aristocrats. By the fourth century the focus of civilian competitive display was the palatial villas in which aristocrats lived as emperors in miniature. However, the reality was that physical, and increasingly ideological, power lay with local multi-ethnic military groups. Dress across the empire was notable for including 'barbarian fashions', such that legislation had to be passed to ensure that the toga was worn in Rome. This situation resulted from the prestige of the army.

Status within the military elite was often expressed in ways associated with a mobile lifestyle, particularly personal dress. Generals and their retinues of the fifth century varied in the degree to which they wanted to embrace Roman civilian models of prestige just as landed aristocrats differed in the degrees to which they were attached to those cultural forms. The failure of the imperial government was to an extent a failure of patronage links between itself and the military elites and landlords. In a situation of insecurity and fragmented landholding, available cash would have been better spent on buying military support than in ostentatious building works which would have been vulnerable to attack.

In the fifth century the western Roman state was weakened and was attempting to make up a deficit in prestige through autocratic decrees and grand ceremonial. The most important battle was in the minds of the subjects. Harris commented concerning the 'fall of the Soviet Empire' (as misleading a phrase as the 'fall of Rome') that 'no amount of thought control could hide the daily reality of long lines to buy food, the endless red tape, the shortages of housing and electricity, and the widespread industrial pollution characteristic of life behind the Iron Curtain'. It has been stated by Hassig that 'the more a hegemonic empire relies on power (the perception that desired goals can be achieved) rather than force (direct physical action), the more efficient it is because the subordinates police themselves. But the costs of compliance must not be perceived as outweighing the benefits: the more exploitative a political system is perceived to be, the more it must rely on force rather than power and the less efficient it becomes.' The perfect autocracy, in other words, is one in which the citizens desire oppression.

The Roman Empire can be seen as a protection racket which extorted money from provincial peasants in order to support a thinly stretched film of aristocrats, army and urbanites. The success of the empire lay in involving countless members of the local population in its wars and its rituals, in its tax system and its world view, and, more particularly, in enabling local elites to join the benefiting group and its culture and so to desire Roman rule. In return security was granted, but when, at the end of antiquity, that was no longer guaranteed, elites could reconsider their own self-interest. Land was the basic resource and its security must always have been the first priority. If the reality of local power in the fifth century was represented by the presence of a Germanic warlord with his retinue, whilst imperial assistance was unlikely, political allegiances could change rapidly and with them associated notions of prestige.

The actions of aristocrats should be considered within the parameters of what was possible and what forms of spending could help them in their social aims. We must expect that notions of what was prestigious would change over time and that classical concepts, for example, had no sure monopoly. Although long possessed of immense power and prestige, the empire and its culture were not inherently superior or automatically perceived as such in the fifth and sixth centuries. The decline of Romanitas in western Europe at the end of antiquity derived substantially from a failure of ideological control. Being culturally Roman had once implied membership of a great empire-wide elite: it now just indicated membership of one ethnic group amongst many. People thought of themselves as Roman and displayed that cultural identity only when they thought it was advantageous to them. Many people simply could have opted out since individuals might take on aspects of 'Roman' or 'barbarian' identities depending on circumstances.

Prestige, during the fifth century, in the face of potential desertion and rebellion of tenants, could be gained by clinging to traditional Romanitas, by establishing relationships with the Church, or by adhering to a 'barbarian' court. Each of these options brought its own distinctive mixture of elite material culture, buildings, books, swords or liturgical silver. The army option has often been associated with Germanic ethnic identity. However, military styles which once seemed barbarian are clearly much more complex products of a mixed society heavily influenced by the traditions of the Roman army. For example, the seemingly 'Dark Age' helmet found at Sutton Hoo is now seen as directly descended in style from late Roman parade helmets. And the garnet jewellery of the early Middle Ages is also seen to have had its origins in Roman regalia, which was itself influenced by Persian and other eastern traditions.

It is easy to leap to 'barbarism' as convenient explanation and description of post-Roman cultural forms. It might be assumed, for instance, that the woman at the Brighthampton cemetery who had a string of ten Roman *denarii* on a necklace was using these coins in a new and barbaric way, but there was, in fact, a lively tradition of wearing coins as jewellery in the Roman world, albeit in settings rather than simply pierced. Continuities with the ancient world sometimes occur in the most unexpected places. The first phase of so-called 'Germanic' art appears to have originated in the hybrid context of the multi-ethnic Roman army. And Matthew Innes, investigating the origins of the Franks, wrote that if we scan the sources for 'indications of the type of origin legend and historical tradition which would nurture a people's identity, we come across one such legend time and time again . . . It is the legend which made the Franks descendants of the Trojans and their rulers descendants of Aeneas.' Indeed, many of the ethnic labels of the early Middle Ages may have had their origins in tribal conglomeration taking place under Roman influence in the late empire: thus, the Franks were welded together as a people by Childeric and his son Clovis; their name and their sense of ethnic identity may, in part, have been imposed upon them by those Romans among whom they lived.

In the light of such complexities it is potentially misleading to write a history based solely on the activities of racial groups and more helpful to consider ethnicities and their associated material cultures as fashions for a purpose, and to measure their influence and spread. Doing this enables us to overcome major difficulties of the traditional explanation of what was going on. For example, because the differences between Roman and Germanic practice cannot be seen as sharply defined we can identify the creation of Anglo-Saxon England without having to imagine the extermination of the Romano-Britons. We can read the situation as a process of cultural dominance of new styles of the display of power. As Hills has commented, 'not only might we be able to detect the previously invisible Britons, still in situ, disguised as very run-down Romans. They might also be disguised as Saxons.'

Prosperity required order. Peace allowed economic growth. When it comes to the survival of elites the fact of order mattered more than who was ensuring it. In Britain the old civilian culture had collapsed into social disorder during the vacuum of patronage and protection with the sudden withdrawal of Roman authority. This led to a rash of silver depositions representing a breakdown in precious metal circulation which was not replicated on anything like that scale on the Continent. The greatest discontinuity came when there was no overlord, German or Roman, to resemble and to grant protection. Moreover, in Britain, there was a lack of powerful church leaders who could act to hold communities together. The Church grew strong in Britain only after the old elite had either vanished or had lost their Romanised material culture. In Gaul the landed elites took over the Church. This gave them prestige and protection on a scale which was apparently not enjoyed in Britain.

Constantine brought Christianity into the cultural forefront of the empire and provided churches with the resources to promote themselves both to the elite and to the masses. The remarkable thing about this process was that there was so little opposition. The Church employed the style of the emperors in art and decoration in order to gain respect, bearing in mind that imperial display was understood as reflecting divinely inspired power. In most cities splendid churches stood as the main public buildings at the end of antiquity and, with the waning of imperial power, this style of art and architecture was left as referring, above all, to spiritual authority. The churches were understood as being images of heaven, and the Church itself was now to be respected not because it was an echo of empire but of paradise.

The picture in relation to secular dwellings was very different. Van Ossel commented on the abandonment of the villa tradition that 'wooden buildings can have the same agricultural capacity as the stone buildings they replace . . . How do we explain this decline in construction *more romanorum* [in the Roman manner]? The answer is complex and not perhaps uniquely dependent on archaeology. It may be a question of disinterest in traditional Roman customs.' I would argue that the elite decoration of secular building was carried out to maintain social position. In circumstances of unstable landholding such main-tenance could best be carried out through displays of power centring on personal attire including grave furnishing, and gifts to subordinates or to the Church. Ostentatious villas were no longer cost-effective.

Peter Brown began his study *The Cult of the Saints* with these words: 'This book is about the joining of Heaven and Earth, and the role, in this joining, of dead human beings.' The relics of martyrs provided the backup of symbolic prestige and supernatural defence. The brilliant Roman styles of elite art and architecture, moreover, were essential to the religious function of churches because they produced, according to Brown, a 'visionary world . . . in which the boundary between body and spirit, death and life, is dissolved in a shimmer of light'. Venantius' captions to the wall paintings commissioned by Gregory for the cathedral of Tours, tell us the images 'would make you think that the coloured figures are alive'. This capacity to bring dead materials to life meant that traditions of Roman art and architecture were desired and could be preserved within the Church even when they had vanished in secular society. Church art and literature derived from the Roman Empire but were now more emblematic of the Christian present than of the imperial past.

8 Summary

This book has examined the way in which, despite its origins, the Church came to replace the State as the main patron of splendour in art and architecture. Christianity originated in the Middle East and expanded slowly through the Jewish and pagan communities of the towns of the region. It started to become prominent in the second century through the actions of martyrs who were put to death in occasional prosecutions for refusing to swear an oath of allegiance which invoked the emperor as associated with the divine. Persecution, such as that ordered by the emperor Decius in 250, alternated with tolerance, since many emperors had other priorities. The main Christian communities at this time were in Syria and the other Near Eastern and North African cities. The Christian population in Britain and the rest of north-western Europe is likely to have been very small indeed, although there is one famous martyr, St Alban. Christianity slowly became an ever more important religious force through the first three centuries AD. But its fortunes were transformed when it was embraced by the emperor Constantine to be the official religion to replace a pagan cult of the imperial person. It is from that age that Christianity emerges into architectural history since it was only then that there was the financial support available to build churches on any scale. Moreover, in earlier periods there were insufficient numbers of Christians for their material culture to show distinctively in the archaeological record.

Classical antiquity was dominated by conservative, land-owning elites. This was the world into which Christianity grew, and which, in many ways, it did little to disturb. Constantine may have been revolutionary in stripping wealth from pagan cults and endowing Christianity, but the general principle of gifts to temples and churches went more or less unquestioned in the late classical world. The Church adopted many of the images as well as the ways of that world. This enabled the new sect to communicate effectively and so to bring about the maximum number of conversions. Many Jewish and pagan religious and secular practices and images were borrowed, though not indiscriminately, and baptised for Christian use. The cautionary words of Jesus, as recorded in the Gospels, were reinterpreted as allegories.

Constantine's actions did not come completely out of the blue. The move toward monotheism and initiatory religions with strong moral codes may be seen throughout the third century. Such religions offered a single explanation for everything, together, in the case of Christianity, with a specific vision of life after death. The government increasingly regarded religious policy as

30 *Vault mosaics, Arian Baptistery, Ravenna. Gold mosaics used expense to show spiritual power and excellence*

important as it meddled in more and more areas of its citizens' lives in the struggle to retain control of its fragmenting empire. From the time when Christianity was promoted as the state cult, the emperor was the lieutenant of God on earth and paganism in all its forms condemned by imperial decree.

As we have seen, precious metals played an important role from Rome to the Middle Ages but the ultimate source of wealth was land. The concentration of agricultural surplus fed workers who could produce the buildings and artefacts with which the elite could display its status. The security of these land-owners varied greatly over time as did their spending power. During the first two centuries AD landed elites in north-western Europe spent a great deal on public urban monuments. With the withdrawal of their military prerogatives their security was dependent upon their status within the Roman system which they were, therefore, keen to demonstrate to each other and to their tenants and other subordinates. The great villas of the fourth century appear to show the apogee of this class, which was now established in control of vast estates on which landowners appeared before their dependants as lords.

This situation changed drastically with the collapse of security from the latter part of the fourth century. Crucially, this process was much more drawn out in Gaul than it was in Britain. Government spending on the British army

31   Details of mosaic of jewelled cross and throne, Arian Baptistery, Ravenna. In late antiquity the cross and the throne were joined rather than in opposition

collapsed, along with the government's tax and spend cycle. Britain sees a wave of silver hoards on a scale unparalleled in Gaul. Yet it was the Continent which appears to have seen a much more substantial Germanic presence at an early date. In many areas of Gaul it seems that aristocratic families were able to negotiate their survival through co-operation with new patrons, even if they were 'barbarian' generals. In southern Britain, however, elite power either vanished temporarily or was only secured by adoption of an entirely new social contract with inferiors which involved a very substantial transfer of surplus wealth to armed followers, leaving far less for noble display. Furthermore, in Gaul aristocrats took over the operation of bishoprics and so bolstered their position within localities and with rulers. The Church was able to protect its property to a considerable degree because of the patronage of the saints. In Gaul, if not in Britain, the Church grew to power during the period of Roman control. The architecture of the late antique world was, therefore, preserved in churches there and became identified with the Christian message.

The Church that finally emerged in the medieval west was in many ways the premier institution to preserve the architecture, dress, rituals and conventions from the ancient world. It did so with such conservatism that modern clerical dress is the direct descendant of Roman garb, whilst the

143

secular shirt and trousers is the direct descendant of close-fitting barbarian dress designed for convenience when horse-riding. The churches of Anglo-Saxon England were designed as remote descendants of the great Roman basilicas. Meanwhile, aristocrats devoted resources to weapons and retinues rather than to maintaining the marble and mosaic grandeur of the ancient world. During the Middle Ages, the Church achieved enhanced social control by establishing ritual jurisdiction over such processes as marriage and death. Certain theologians suggested that the worldly realm, including its reserves of wealth, which was the creation of God, should rightly come under the governance of the Church. Critics of such grandiose designs pointed to the suggested 'purity' of the early (poor) Christians which was based, ultimately, on the modesty of Christ himself. It is an issue that strikes at the heart of Christianity, a religion which was never, and perhaps can never be, *entirely* at ease with the physical world.

Further reading

The suggested texts do not, between them, examine all the things I have been talking about. They represent directions in which to progress in exploring aspects of the ancient world which are covered in this book. They have been selected for being accessible and for being both engaging as well as informative.

Donald Kyle, *Spectacles of Death in Ancient Rome* (London, 1998), explores the world of the arena, gladiators and executions. For a general religious background to the ancient world, Ramsay MacMullen, *Paganism in the Roman Empire* (New Haven, 1981). Also useful, by the same author, are *Christianising the Roman Empire (AD 100-400)* (New Haven, 1984) and *Constantine* (London, 1987).

Other overviews of Christianisation are W.H.C. Frend, *The Rise of Christianity* (London, 1984) and Rodney Stark, *The Rise of Christianity: A Sociologist Reconsiders History* (Princeton, 1996). Robert Wilken, *The Christians as Romans Saw Them* (London, 1984), is a useful corrective to Christian-centric accounts.

Original texts are most obviously available in the Bible narratives of the Gospels and Acts of the Apostles. The story is followed through to the fourth century in Eusebius, *A History of the Church from Christ to Constantine*, of which there are various editions, but the easiest to find is the Penguin Classics Paperback (Harmondsworth, 1965).

A short and well-illustrated introduction to the later Roman period is Peter Brown, *The World of Late Antiquity: From Marcus Aurelius to Muhammad* (London, 1971). Sabine McCormack, *Art and Ceremony in Late Antiquity* (Berkeley, 1981) and Michael McCormick, *Eternal Victory: Triumphal Rulership in Late Antiquity, Byzantium, and the Early Medieval West* (Cambridge, 1986), are interesting to compare as parallel studies in power, display and government.

This current book stems from the academic research I carried out for my PhD which was published in revised form as Dominic Janes, *God and Gold in Late Antiquity* (Cambridge, 1998). The archaeological evidence for the fate of the north-western provinces of Rome is most clearly interpreted by Simon Esmonde Cleary, *The Ending of Roman Britain* (London, 1991). Perhaps the best primary source for the post-Roman west is Gregory of Tours, *History of the Franks*, L. Thorpe (trans.) (Harmondsworth, 1974). For a vivid account of the wider processes at work across Europe, the period piece, Edward Gibbon, *Decline and Fall of the Roman Empire*, remains a classic. It is available in many versions, but the abridgement which is to be recommended is the Penguin Paperback edited by David Womersley (Harmondsworth, 2000).

Bibliography

This is a list of some of the more important works which were consulted in the writing of this book. It is intended to help you in following up references to modern authors in the text. Ancient sources are often available only in scholarly editions and so I have not provided a separate list of these. But major university libraries will have good editions available.

Alcock, L. (1963) *Dinas Powys: An Iron Age, Dark Age and Early Medieval Settlement in Glamorgan* (Cardiff)
    (1987) *Economy, Society and Warfare among the Britons and Saxons* (Cardiff)
    (1995) *Cadbury Castle, Somerset: The Early Medieval Archaeology* (Cardiff)
Archambault, P.J. (1990) 'Gregory of Tours and the classical tradition', in A. S. Bernardo & S. Levin (eds) *The Classics in the Middle Ages: Papers of the Twentieth Annual Conference of the Center for Medieval and Early Renaissance Studies*, Medieval and Renaissance Texts and Studies 69 (Binghamton, N.Y), pp.25-34
Arnheim, M.T.W. (1972) *The Senatorial Aristocracy in the Later Roman Empire* (Oxford)
Atsma, H. (ed.) (1989) *La Neustrie: Les pays au nord de la Loire de 650 à 850: Colloque historique international*, Beihefte der Francia 16, 2 vols (Sigmaringen)
Auerbach, E. (1953) *Mimesis: The Representation of Reality in Western Literature*, trans. W.R. Trask (Princeton)
    (1993) *Literary Language and its Public in Late Latin Antiquity and in the Middle Ages*, trans. R. Manheim, BS 74 (Princeton)
Ausenda G. (ed.) (1995) *After Empire: Towards an Ethnology of Europe's Barbarians*, Studies in Historical Archaeoethnology 1 (Woodbridge)
Axboe, M. & Kromann, A. (1992) 'DN ODINN P F AUC? Germanic "imperial portraits" on Scandinavian gold bracteates', *Acta Hyperborea* 4, pp.271-306
Balmelle, C. (1985) *La décor géométrique de la mosaïque romaine: repertoire graphique et descriptif des compositions linéaires et isotropes* (Paris)
    (1993) 'Le repértoire végétal de mosaïques du sud-ouest de la Gaule et des sculpteurs des sarcophages dits d'Aquitaine', *Antiquité Tardive* 1, pp.101-9
    (1996) 'Le décor en mosaïque des édifaces des sud-ouest de la Gaule dans l'antiquité tardive', in Maurin & Pailler (1996), pp.193-208

Bammesburger, A. & Wollmann, A. (eds) (1990) *Britain, 400-600: Language and History*, Anglistische Forschungen 205 (Heidelberg)

Baratte, F. (1975) 'Les ateliers d'argenterie au bas-empire', *Journal des savants*, pp.193-212

(ed.) (1988) *Argenterie Romaine et Byzantine* (Paris)

(1992) 'Les trésors de temples dans le monde romain: une expression particulière de la piété', in Boyd & Mango (1992), pp.111-21

Baratte, F. & Painter, K. (eds) (1989) *Trésors d'orfèvrerie Gallo-Romains* (Paris)

Barley, M.W. & Hanson, R.P.C. (eds) (1968) *Christianity in Britain, 300-700* (Leicester)

Barnes, T.D. (1981) *Constantine and Eusebius* (Cambridge, Mass.)

Barnish, S. (1988) 'The transformation and survival of the western senatorial aristocracy', *Publications of the British School at Rome* 56, pp.120-55

(1989) 'The transformation of classical cities and the Pirenne debate', *Journal of Roman Archaeology* 2, pp.385-400

Barral I Altet, X. (1991) 'La mosaïque', in Duval, Fontaine & Février (1991), pp.238-48

(1989) 'Le décor des monuments religieux de Neustrie', in Atsma 2 pp.209-24

Beard, M. & North, J. (eds) (1990) *Pagan Priests: Religion and Power in the Ancient World* (London)

Beard, M., North, J. & Price, S. (1998) *Religions of Rome*, 2 vols (Cambridge)

Beckwith, J. (1970) *Early Christian and Byzantine Art* (Harmondsworth)

Bell, T. (1998) 'Churches on Roman buildings: Christian associations and Roman masonry in Anglo-Saxon England', *Medieval Archaeology* 42, pp.1-18

Black, E.W. (1994) 'Villa owners, Romano-British gentlemen and officers', *Britannia* 25, pp.99-111

Bloch, H. (1963) 'The pagan revival in the west at the end of the fourth century', in A. Momigliano (ed.) *The Conflict Between Paganism and Christianity in the Fourth Century* (Oxford, 1963), pp.193-218

Borger, J. (1996) 'Muslim returnees open Pandora's box', *The Guardian*, 30 September, p.11

Boyd, S.A. & Mango, M.M. (eds) (1992) *Ecclesiastical Silver Plate in Sixth-Century Byzantium* (Washington)

Branigan, K. (1977) *The Roman Villa in South-West England* (Bradford on Avon)

(1980) *Roman Britain: Life in an Imperial Province* (London)

Branigan, K. & Miles, D. (eds) (1995) *The Economies of Romano-British Villas: Economic Aspects of Romano-British Villas* (Sheffield)

Brennan, B. (1992) 'The image of the Merovingian bishop in the poetry of Venantius Fortunatus', *Journal of Medieval History* 18, pp.115-39

Breukelaar, A.H.B. (1994) *Historiography and Episcopal Authority in Sixth-Century Gaul: The Histories of Gregory of Tours Interpreted in their Historical Context*, Forschungen zur Kirchen- und Dogmengeschichte 57 (Göttingen)

Brown, P.R.L. (1971) *The World of Late Antiquity: From Marcus Aurelius to Muhammad* (London)

(1980) 'Art and society in Late Antiquity', in Weitzman (1980), pp.17-28

(1981) *The Cult of the Saints* (Chicago)

(1982) *Society and the Holy in Late Antiquity* (London)

(1987) 'Late Antiquity', in Veyne (1987), pp.235-311

(1990) 'Bodies and minds: sexuality and renunciation in early Christianity', in D.M. Halperin, J.J. Winckler & F.I. Zeitlin (eds) *Before Sexuality: The Construction of Erotic Experience in the Ancient Greek World* (Princeton), pp.479-93

(1992) *Power and Persuasion in Late Antiquity: Towards a Christian Empire* (Madison)

(1996) *The Rise of Western Christendom: Triumph and Diversity AD 200-1000* (London)

(1997) 'The world of late Antiquity revisited', *Symbolae Osloensis* 72, pp.5-30

(2000) 'The study of elites in late Antiquity', *Arethusa* 33, pp.321-46

Cookson, N. (1984) *Romano-British Mosaics: A Reassessment and Critique of some Notable Stylistic Affinities*, BAR, BS 135 (Oxford)

Burnett, A. (1984) 'Clipped *siliquae* and the end of Roman Britain', *Britannia* 15, pp.163-8

(1987) *Coinage in the Roman World* (London)

Cabot, J. & Meyer, D. (1995) *Sorde-L'Abbeye* (Dax)

Caillet, J.-P. (1993) *L'évergétisme monumental chrétien en Italie et à ses marges: D'après l'épigraphie des pavements de mosaïque (IVe – VIIe s.)* (Rome)

Cameron, Averil (1991) *Christianity and the Rhetoric of Empire: The Development of Christian Discourse*, Sather Classical Lectures 55 (Berkeley)

(1993) *The Later Roman Empire, A.D. 284-430* (London)

(1993) *The Mediterranean World in Late Antiquity, A.D. 395-600* (London)

Corbett, J.H. (1981) 'The saint as patron in the work of Gregory of Tours', *Journal of Medieval History* 7, pp.1-13

Courcelle, P. (1964) *Histoire littéraire des grandes invasions germaniques*, 3rd ed. (Paris)

Crook, J. (2000) *The Architectural Setting of the Cult of Saints in the Early Medieval West, C. 300-1200* (Oxford)

Cookson, N. (1984) *Romano-British Mosaics: A Reassessment and Critique of some Notable Stylistic Affinities*, British Archaeological Reports, British Series 135 (Oxford)

(1986-7) 'The Christian church in Roman Britain: a synthesis of archaeology', *World Archaeology* 18, pp.426-33

Daniélou, J. (1953) 'Terre et paradis chez les Péres de l'Église', *Eranos Yearbook* 22, pp.433-72

Dark, K.R. (1994) *'Civitas' to Kingdom: British Political Continuity 300-800* (London)

Delmaire, R. (1977) 'La caisse des largesses sacrées et l'armée au bas–empire', in *Armées et fiscalité dans le monde antique*, Colloques nationaux du Centre National de la Recherche Scientifique 936 (Paris), pp.311-29

Depeyrot, G. (1987) *La bas empire Romain: Economie et numismatique (284-491)* (Paris)

(1991) *Crises et inflation entre antiquité et Moyen Age* (Paris)

(1994) *Richesse et société chez les Mérovingiens et Carolingiens* (Paris)

De Ste Croix, G.E.M. (1975) 'Early Christian attitudes to property and slavery', in D. Baker (ed.) (1975) *Church, Society and Politics*, Studies in Church History 12 (Oxford), pp.1-38

Dorigo, W. (1971) *Late Roman Painting* (London)

Douglas, M. & Isherwood, B. (1996) *The World of Goods: Toward an Anthropology of Consumption*, 2nd edition (London)

Drinkwater, J. & Elton, H. (eds) (1992) *Fifth-Century Gaul: A Crisis of Identity* (Cambridge)

Dumville, D.N. (1977) 'Sub-Roman Britain: history and legend', *History* 62, pp.173-92

Dunbabin, K.M.D. (1978) *The Mosaics of Roman North Africa: Studies in Iconography and Patronage* (Oxford)

(1999) *Mosaics of the Greek and Roman World* (Cambridge)

Duncan-Jones, R. (1982) *The Economy of the Roman Empire: Quantitative Studies* (Cambridge)

Duval, N., Fontaine, J., Février, P.-A. *et al.* (eds) (1991*) Naissance des arts chrétiens: atlas des monuments paléolchrétiens de la France* (Paris)

Duval, N., Fontaine, J., Février, P.-A. *et al.* (eds) (1995-8) *Les premiers monuments chrétiens de la France*, 3 vols (Paris)

Ellis, S. P. (1988) 'The end of the Roman house', *American Journal of Archaeology* 92, pp.565-76

(1991) 'Power, architecture and decor: how the late Roman aristocrat appeared to his guests', in E.K. Gazda (ed.) *Roman Art in the Private Sphere: New Perspectives on the Architecture and Decor of the Domus, Villa and Insula* (Ann Arbor), pp.117-37

Elsner, J. (1995) *Art and the Roman Viewer: The Transformation of Art from the Pagan World to Christianity* (Cambridge)

Esler, P.F. (ed.) (2000) *The Early Christian World*, 2 vols (London)

Esmonde Cleary, S. (1989) *The Ending of Roman Britain* (London)

Farwell, D.E. & Molleson, T.I. (1993) *Excavations at Poundbury*, vol. 2 (of 2), *The Cemeteries* (Dorchester)

Finney, P.C. (1994) *The Invisible God: The Earliest Christians on Art* (New York)

Flower, H. (1996) *Ancestor Masks and Aristocratic Power in Roman Culture* (Oxford)

Frere, S.S. (1987) *Britannia: A History of Roman Britain*, 3rd ed. (London)

Garnsey, P. & Saller, R. (1987) *The Roman Empire: Economy, Society and Culture* (London)

George, E.W. (1992) *Venantius Fortunatus: A Latin Poet in Merovingian Gaul* (Cambridge)

Gerson, L.P. (1994) *Plotinus* (London)

Gibbon, E. (1994) *The History of the Decline and Fall of the Roman Empire*, 3 vols, D. Womersley (ed.) (London)

Gilliard, F.D. (1979) 'The senators of sixth-century Gaul', *Speculum* 54, pp.685-97

Girouard, M. (1980) *Life in the English Country House: A Social and Architectural History* (Harmondsworth)

Godman, P. (1987) *Poets and Emperors: Frankish Politics and Carolingian Poetry* (Oxford)

Goffart, W. (1988) *The Narrators of Barbarian History (A.D. 550-800): Jordanes, Gregory of Tours, Bede, and Paul the Deacon* (Princeton)
(1989) *Rome's Fall and After* (London)

Golomstock, I. (1990) *Totalitarian Art in the Soviet Union, the Third Reich, Fascist Italy and the People's Republic of China*, R. Chaneller (trans.) (London)

Gombrich, E.H. (1984) *The Sense of Order: A Study in the Psychology of Decorative Art*, 2nd ed. (London)

Goodenough, E.R. (1953-68) *Jewish Symbols in the Graeco-Roman Period*, Bollingen Series 37 (New York), 13 vols

Grabar, A.N. (1936) *L'émpereur dans l'art Byzantin: Recherches sur l'art officiel de l'empire d'orient*, Publications de la faculté des lettres de l'Université de Strasbourg 75 (Paris)

Gregson, M.S. (1982) 'The villa as private property in Roman Britain', in K.W. Ray (ed.) (1982) *Young Archaeologist: Collected Unpublished Papers, Mark S. Gregson* (Cambridge), pp.143-91

Halsberghe, G.H. (1972) *The Cult of 'Sol Invictus'* (Leiden)

Harries, J. (1984) '"Treasure in heaven": property and inheritance among senators of late Rome', in E.M. Craik (ed.) (1984) *Marriage and Property* (Aberdeen), pp.54-70
(1994) *Sidonius Apollinaris and the Fall of Rome, A.D. 407-485* (Oxford)

Harris, M. (1997) *Culture, People, Nature: An Introduction to General Anthropology*, 7th ed. (New York)

Hassig, R. (1990) 'Aztec warfare', *History Today* 40, February, pp.17-24

Haverfield, F. (1923) *The Romanisation of Roman Britain*, 4th ed. (Oxford)

Heather, P. (1994) 'Literacy and power in the Migration Period', A.K. Bowman & G. Woolf (eds) *Literacy and Power in the Ancient World* (Cambridge), pp.177-97

Heinzelmann, M. (1976) *Bisschofsherrschaft in Gallien: Zur Continuität römischer Führungsschichten vom 4 bis 7 Jahrhundert: Soziale, prosopografische und bildungsgeschichtliche Aspekte* (Munich)
(1994) *Gregor von Tours (538-594): 'Zehn Bücher Geschichte': Historiographie und Gesellschaftskonzept im 6. Jahrhundert* (Darmstadt)

Heuclin, J. (1988) *Aux origines monastiques de la Gaule du Nord: ermites et reclus du Ve au XIe siècle* (Lille)

Higham, N. (1992) *Rome, Britain and the Anglo-Saxons* (London)
(1994) *The English Conquest: Gildas and Britain in the Fifth Century* (Manchester)

Hobbs, R. (1997) 'Late Roman precious metal deposits, *c.*AD 200-700: changes over time and space', London University PhD dissertation
(1997) 'The Mildenhall treasure: Roald Dahl's ultimate tale of the unexpected?' *Antiquity* 71, pp.63-73

Hobsbawm, E.J. (1969) *Bandits* (London)

Innes, M.J. (2000) 'Teutons or Trojans? The Carolingians and the Germanic past', in Y. Hen & Innes, (eds) *The Uses of the Past in the Early Middle Ages* (Cambridge), pp.227-49

Janes, D. (1998) *God and Gold in Late Antiquity* (Cambridge)

Johns, C. & Bland, R. (1995) *The Hoxne Treasure: An Illustrated Introduction* (London)

Johns, C. & Potter, T. (1983) *The Thetford Treasure: Roman Jewellery and Silver* (London)

Kerlouégan, F. (1987) *Le 'De Excidio Britanniae' de Gildas: Les destinées de la culture latine dans l'île de Bretagne au VIe siècle* (Paris)

Kessler, H.L. (1985) 'Pictorial narrative and church mission in sixth-century Gaul', in Kessler & M.S. Simpson (1985) *Pictorial Narrative in Antiquity and the Middle Ages*, Studies in the History of Art, 16, pp.75-91

Kitzinger, E. (1954) 'The cult of images in the age before iconoclasm', *Dumbarton Oaks Papers* 8, pp.83-150

Lane Fox, R. (1986) *Pagans and Christians* (London)

Lapidge, M. & Dumville, D. (eds) (1984) *Gildas: New Approaches*, Studies in Celtic History 5 (Woodbridge)

Lewin, L. (1979) 'The oligarchical limitations of social banditry in Brazil: the case of the "good" thief, Antonio Silvino', *Past and Present* 82, pp.116-46

Lewis, G. (1980) *The Day of Shining Red: An Essay on Understanding Ritual*, Cambridge Studies in Social Anthropology 27 (Cambridge)

Ling, R. (1991) *Roman Painting* (Cambridge)

L'Orange, H.P. (1965) *Art Forms and Civic Life in the Later Roman Empire* (Princeton)

MacCormack, S.G. (1981) *Art and Ceremony in Late Antiquity*, Transformation of the Classical Heritage 1 (Berkeley)
(1991) *Religion in the Andes: Vision and Imagination in Early Colonial Peru* (Princeton)

McCormick, M. (1986) *Eternal Victory: Triumphal Rulership in Late Antiquity, Byzantium, and the Early Medieval West* (Cambridge)

MacMullen, R. (1981) *Paganism in the Roman Empire* (New Haven)
(1997) *Christianity and Paganism in the Fourth to Eighth Centuries* (Yale)

Maguire, E.D. & H.P. & Duncan-Flowers, M.J. (1989) *Art and Holy Powers in the Early Christian House*, Illinois Byzantine Studies 2 (Urbana)

Maguire, H.P. (1987) *Earth and Ocean: The Terrestrial World in Early Byzantine Art*, Monographs on the Fine Arts 43 (University Park)

Mango, C. (1980) *Byzantium: The Empire of New Rome* (London)

Mathews, T.F. (1993) *The Clash of Gods: A Reinterpretation of Early Christian Art* (Princeton)

Maurin, L. & Pailler, J.-M. (eds) (1996) *Le civilisation urbaine de l'antiquité tardive dans le sud-ouest de la Gaule*, Aquitania 14 (Bordeaux)

Miles, D. (ed.) (1982) *The Romano-British Countryside: Studies in Rural Settlement and Society*, British Archaeological Reports, British Series 103 (Oxford)

Miles, R. (ed.) (1999) *Constructing Identities in Late Antiquity* (London)

Murray, A.C. (ed.) (1998) *After Rome's Fall: Narrators and Sources of Early Medieval History: Essays Presented to Walter Goffart* (Toronto)

Painter, K.S. (1971) 'Villas and Christianity in Roman Britain', *British Museum Quarterly* 35, pp.157-75

Percival, J. (1976) *The Roman Villa: An Historical Introduction* (London)

Pietri, C. (1978) 'Evergetisme et richesses ecclésiastiques dans l'Italie du IVe à la fin du Ve s.: l'exemple romain', *Ktema* 3, pp.317-37

(1981) 'Donations et pieux établissements d'après le légendier romain (Ve – VIIe s.)', in (1981) *Hagiographie, cultures et sociétés, IVe – XIIe siècles: Actes du colloque organisé à Nanterre et à Paris (2-5 Mai 1979)* (Paris), pp.435-53

Porter, R. (1988) *Gibbon* (London)

Price, S.R.F. (1984) *Rituals and Power: The Roman Imperial Cult in Asia Minor* (Cambridge)

Randsborg, K. (ed.) (1989) *The Birth of Europe: Archaeology and Social Development in the First Millenium A.D.*, Analecta Romana Instituti Danici, Suppl. 16 (Rome)

Rees, B.R. (1988) *Pelagius: A Reluctant Heretic* (Woodbridge)

Reinhold, M. (1970) *History of Purple as a Status Symbol in Antiquity*, Collection Latomus 116 (Brussels)

Rheinisches Landesmuseum, Trier (1984) *Trier: Kaiserresidenz und Bischofssitz: Die Stadt in spätantike und frühchristliche Zeit* (Mainz)

Rich, J. (ed.) (1992) *The City in Late Antiquity*, Leicester-Nottingham Studies in Ancient Society 3 (London)

Roberts, M. (1989) *The Jewelled Style: Poetry and Poetics in Late Antiquity* (Ithaca)

Salzman, M.R. (2000) 'Elite realities and "mentalités": The making of a western Christian aristocracy', *Arethusa* 33, pp.347-62

Samson, R. (1987) 'A Merovingian nobleman's home: villa or castle?', *Journal of Medieval History* 13, pp.287-315

Sear, F.B. (1977) *Roman Wall and Vault Mosaics* (Heidelberg)

Small, A. (ed.) (1996) *Subject and Ruler: The Cult of the Ruling Power in Classical Antiquity*, Journal of Roman Archaeology, Supplementary Series 17 (Ann Arbor)

Smith, R.R.R. (1988) *Hellenistic Ruler Portraits* (Oxford)

Stancliffe, C.E. (1983) *St. Martin and his Hagiographer: History and Miracle in Sulpicius Severus* (Oxford)

Stark, R. (1996) *The Rise of Christianity: A Sociologist Reconsiders History* (Princeton)

Straub, J.A. (1967) 'Constantine as *Koinoe Epiekopoe*: tradition and innovation in the representation of the first Christian Emperor's majesty', *Dumbarton Oaks Papers* 21 pp.37-55

Stroheker, K.F. (1941) 'Die Senatoren bei Gregor von Tours', *Klio* 16, pp.293-305

(1948) *Die senatorische Adel im spätantiken Gallien* (Tübingen)

Strong, D.E. (1966) *Greek and Roman Silver Plate* (London)

Stupperich, R. (1980) 'A reconsideration of some fourth-century British mosaics', *Britannia* 11, pp.289-301

Swift, E. (2000) *The End of the Western Roman Empire: An Archaeological Investigation* (Stroud)

Tainter, J. (1988) *The Collapse of Complex Societies* (Cambridge)

Thébert, Y. (1987) 'Private life and domestic architecture in Roman Africa', in Veyne (1987), pp.313-409

Thompson, E.A. (1982) *Barbarians and Romans: The Decline of the Western Empire* (Wisconsin)

(1983) 'Fifth-century facts?' *Britannia* 14, pp.272-4

(1984) *Saint Germanus of Auxerre and the End of Roman Britain* (Woodbridge)

Van Dam, R. (1985) *Leadership and Community in Late Antique Gaul*, Transformation of the Classical Heritage 8 (Berkeley)

(1993) *Saints and their Miracles in Late Antique Gaul* (Princeton)

Van Ossel, P. (1992) *Etablissements ruraux de l'Antiquité tardive dans le nord de la Gaule*, Supplément à Gallia 51 (Paris)

& Ouzoulias, P. (2000) 'Rural settlement economy in Northern Gaul in the late empire: An overview and assessment', *Journal of Roman Archaeology* 13, pp.133-60

Veyne, P. (1976) *Le pain et le cirque* (Paris)

(ed.) (1987) *From Pagan Rome to Byzantium*, A History of Private Life (5 vols., P. Ariès & G. Duby (eds)) 1 (Cambridge, Mass.)

Vieillard-Troiekouroff, M. (1976) *Les monuments religieux de la Gaule d'apres les oeuvres de Grégoire de Tours* (Paris)

Ward-Perkins, B. (1984) *From Classical Antiquity to the Middle Ages: Urban Public Building in Northern and Central Italy, A.D. 300-850* (Oxford)

Watts, D. (1991) *Christians and Pagans in Roman Britain* (London)
   (1998) *Religion in Late Roman Britain: Forces of Change* (London)
Webster, L. & Backhouse, J. (eds) (1991) *The Making of England: Anglo-Saxon Art and Culture, A.D. 600-900* (London)
Webster, L. & Brown, M. (eds) (1997) *The Transformation of the Roman World, AD 400-900* (London)
Weidemann, M. (1982) *Kulturgeschichte der Merowingerzeit nach den Werken Gregor von Tours*, 2 vols (Mainz)
Weitzmann, K. (ed.) (1979) *Age of Spirituality: Late Antique and Early Christian Art, Third to Seventh Century* (New York)
   (ed.) (1980) *Age of Spirituality: A Symposium* (New York)
White, L.M. (1990) *Building God's Home in the Roman World: Architectural Adaptation Among Pagans, Jews and Christians* (Baltimore)
Whittaker, C.R. (1994) *Frontiers of the Roman Empire: A Social and Economic Study* (Baltimore)
Wightman, E.M. (1970) *Roman Trier and the Treveri* (London)
   (1985) *Gallia Belgica* (London)
Wilson, R.J.A. (1983) *Piazza Armerina* (Austin)
Wood, I.N. (1986) 'The audience of architecture in post-Roman Gaul', in A.S. Butler & R. Morris (eds) (1986) *The Anglo-Saxon Church: Papers in Honour of Dr H.M. Taylor*, Council for British Archaeology, Research Report 60 (London), pp.74-79
Woodward, A. & Leach, P. (1990) *The Uley Shrines: Excavation of a Ritual Complex on West Hill, Uley, Gloucestershire, 1977-9* (London)
Woolf, G. (1996) 'The uses of forgetfulness in Roman Gaul', in Gehrke, H.-J. & Möller, A. (eds) (1996) *Vergangenheit und Lebenswelt: Soziale Kommunikation, Traditionsbildung und historisches Bewusstsein* (Tübingen)
   (1998) *Becoming Roman: The Origins of Provincial Civilisation in Gaul* (Cambridge)
Woolf, R. (1976) 'The idea of men dying with their lord in the *Germania* and in the *Battle of Malden*', *Anglo-Saxon England* 5, pp.63-81
Wormald, P. (1976) 'The decline of the Western Empire and the survival of its aristocracy', *Journal of Roman Studies* 66, pp.217-26
Yoffee, N. & Cowgill, G.L. (eds) *The Collapse of Ancient States and Civilisations* (Tucson)
Zanker, P. (1995) *The Mask of Socrates: The Image of the Intellectual in Antiquity*, trans. A. Shapiro, Sather Classical Lectures 59 (Berkeley)

Index

Certain entries – Rome, Romans, for instance – are mentioned too often to be usefully indexed. In general ancient writers have been given below but not modern ones